THE
BEAT GAME
"The Truth About Hip-Hop Production"

DARRELL "DIGGA" BRANCH

BRANCH FAMILY
PUBLISHING

DEDICATION

This book is dedicated to the loving memory of my grandfather Alfred H. Avant Sr., my grandmother Barbara Branch, my great grandmother Lillian Avant and my music partner and friend Derek "Bloodshed" Armstead.

For information:

E-mail: orders@branchfamilypublishing.com.

This book is printed on acid-free paper.

Printed in the United States of America.

Illustrations by Darrell "Digga" Branch, New York, NY

Typesetter/Designer	Darrell Branch
Cover Designer	Darrell Branch
Editor	Adiyemi Prowell

TABLE OF CONTENTS

ACKNOWLEDGMENTS

There is no possible way I could have written this book without the help and encouragement from my wife Monica and children, Jordan and Darrell. I would like to thank my loving parents Giselle Avant and Darrell Branch for their unconditional support. I want to acknowledge and thank all the following people for their inspiration, insight and help: The Avant family, the Branch family, the Wheeler family, the Nicholson family, the Willis family, the Huckaby family, the Harris family, the Dixon family, the Salters family, Lance "Un" Rivera and family, Renaissance Leadership Academy, my professional colleagues at the Department of Education and in the entertainment industry.

Preface

Nobel and Pulitzer Prize-winning American novelist Toni Morrison once said, "If there's a book you really want to read, but it hasn't been written yet, then you must write it." That single quote is what inspired me to write this book. My love and respect for music has not only inspired me to share my experiences and knowledge within this book, it has lead me on my own path of self-discovery. During my sixteen-year professional journey I've discovered that because of music, I'm able to help others communicate through artistic expression. A person may have a song idea in his or her mind but lack the skill or knowhow of turning the idea into something tangible. However, I can listen to his or her idea and convert it into a music composition. Before attempting to write this book, I felt it was necessary to rediscover why specific elements in Hip-Hop production were important to the music Hip-Hop genre. After reflecting and gaining a renewed understanding of Hip-Hop production, I made a commitment to deliver my honest perspective and personal truth about "The Beat Game."

Producers are specialists in communicating vision. Vision is a thought or concept formed by our imagination. After doing some self-evaluating, I discovered that my passion to become a music producer derived from being a visionary. I believe I have a keen ability to see beyond what others may envision. I understood at a young age that music production would be my passion in life. As a producer, I'm able to take musical pieces of a puzzle and put them together to create the perfect picture. That process continues to excite me today. This book allows me to share my experience and wisdom as an educational resource.

I received further confirmation of why I needed to write this book when I received an email from a young aspiring beat maker from Africa in 2004. He received my contact information and website address located in the production credit liner notes of the 2003 album *Get Rich Or Die Tryin'* by Hip-Hop artist 50 Cent. The young man's email contained some intriguing questions about production and the business of music. What especially fascinated me was not just his questions, but also his reason to reach out to me for knowledge from across the world. That single email changed the direction of my professional career to focus on delivering music education internationally through online sites, music conferences, music programs, books and publications. Through the creation of these sites and music programs I have tutored and mentored people from all around the world.

There are great books on the market that focus on music production. I've gone further and have developed a resource that delivers information based on real world scenarios and experiences within the Hip-Hop industry. It is important to provide aspiring beat makers and producers with not only the information they *want to know* about music production but also the information they *need* to know to be successful in field of Hip-Hop production.

The Beat Game provides a basic framework of the Hip-Hop music production industry. To give you a summary of Hip-Hop production, this book is divided into two sections:

Part One is an overview of the most important areas in the music production field. Areas of interest include: Creating your Dream Team, and gaining knowledge to handle: management, finance, legal issues, publishing, royalties, sampling and more.

Part Two is a guide to help aspiring beat makers, producers and musicians who need "winning strategies" in communication, inspiration, networking, leadership, trade marking your name, rules when working in the studio and more.

Let's get the game started!

The Breakthrough

"Within an instant, the energy in the room changed. My music came through the speakers so loud and crystal clear."

My life in Hip-Hop music began on December 25, 1984. Many people may have difficulty remembering gifts they received on Christmas over 25 years ago, but I remember them vividly. Under the Christmas tree were three boxes. In them was a set of Gemini turntables and a stereo mixer. The gifts that came from my mother and uncle who was a Hip-Hop disc jockey at the time would forever change my life. He introduced me to Hip-Hop music and the art of Deejaying. Over a two-year period, I learned different techniques like blending, mixing, scratching and music selection. My uncle had an extensive record collection, which helped me develop the knowledge and appreciation for different genres. Disco, Soul, Calypso and Rock N Roll were all genres I became familiar with. At the age of nine, I remember listening intently for specific elements in music like drum solos, piano riffs and horn hits. This helped me distinguish similarities and differences between music genres. As a producer, it is important to develop the skill of *listening*. Having listening skills allow you to deconstruct songs and put them back together like pieces of a musical puzzle. When I discovered the skill of listening, I was encouraged to go on and develop into much more than an aspiring disc jockey.

The following year at Christmas, I asked my mom for more pieces to add to my electronic "toy chest." I nagged her for two straight months about buying me electronic equipment from a local electronic store. When Christmas finally came around again, I received some clothing, a large Trans-Am convertible car and two other gifts that made me extremely excited. My mom got me the Mattel Synsonics Drums and a Casio SK-1 Keyboard. At the time, those items were the only affordable and obtainable beat making tools available for beginner aspiring beat makers like myself. In comparison, kids my age requested He-Man action figures and Voltron toys but I had a different focus. At the age of ten, I was intent on putting together my own production workstation. My focus was primarily on becoming a beat maker. To this day, the Casio SK-1 still triggers great memories for me. I still have one and in my studio. It serves as a visual reminder of my early sampling days. As for the Trans-Am car, it stayed in topnotch condition, as I had never played with it.

As a nine year old I started collecting deejay equipment. As a ten year old, I started exploring making sounds and sampling music. The more I learned about music, the more intrigued I became by it. After having a conversation with my grandfather at the kitchen table in 1986, I realized that all the information I had been absorbing over the past two years was leading me into the world of music production. My grandfather was an artist, producer and owner of his own record label during the 1960s. After getting a brief lesson about the inner-workings of the music industry from him, he mentioned one thing that really stood out to me. "The producer is the one that puts everything together. They're the ones who assemble the artist, musicians and engineers to make a hit." The job title "music producer" immediately captured my attention. Until that moment, I thought the artist who was solely responsible for delivering every aspect of a song. It never occurred to me that there were other people involved in the creation of music. From this enlightening conversation, I realized for the first time in my life, I could use my talents to make music with others.

I made the leap into the world of music production in seventh grade. I didn't know exactly what I was in for when I made that decision but I knew I wanted to create Hip-Hop music. Of course, the fame, the fortune and the girls was a hopeful bonus of making music. This was around the time when Hip-Hop group Naughty By Nature were popular, and all the girls loved the lead rapper Treach. I was more interested in the creation of the music, but I must admit, I was a little jealous because it appeared that the rappers got all the attention. The pressure to become a rapper was heavy at the time which is why I decided to do both, rap and produce. I began developing two crafts, my production skills and my own individual rap style. I was so intrigued by Hip-Hop that I dedicated my life to studying the genre inside and out.

My love for music production continued to develop as I began to work with my neighborhood friends Derek Armstead and Cameron Giles. We shared a mutual bond, which was our love for Hip-Hop. I was ready to make contributions showing my skills as a beat maker as well as a rapper. I was a very good rapper too! But my heart was truly into music production. I took more interest and studied more intently on learning how producers Large Professor programmed drums and Diamond D chopped up samples. I was more interested in the development aspect of music rather than lyric writing, which my friends accepted as an important part of our development as Hip-Hop artists. Although I wasn't a primary lyric writer, with our combined talents Cameron, Derek and I went on to form a Hip-Hop group called Caged Fury with hopes of landing a major record deal.

As a teen, I didn't have enough money to buy recording equipment on my own. I received financial allowances from family members. Most of the time, I would use my entire allowance to pay for studio time at neighborhood recording studios. For forty dollars, I would use the equipment at the studio to make beats for the group in less than two hours. Being the group's producer and not having any professional musical equipment at home was stressful. I didn't have much experience using the equipment in studios, nor could I consistently practice and build up my skills. Most of time, my only option was to somehow prepare my musical ideas before I arrived. The restrictions of not having a studio was a huge limitation for me, but played an important role in my development as a producer. It forced me to think critically about every element of the song in advance in my head. *If I put this part with this part, will it work? How would this sound together? Is it possible to slow the sample down?* I started to listen to old recordings and imagine creative ways to manipulate elements from a song to create something new.

To make sense of it, in my mind I would break the song up into a puzzle. Then I would switch around or reorganize the original arrangement of the song. After formulating numerous options in my head I would then try them out in the studio hoping that one of my ideas would translate into a *banging* track. When I began to replicate my ideas using samplers in the studio (we'll talk about sampling on page 123), the musical puzzles I would formulate came together loud and clear through the speakers. I'm proud to say that nine times out of ten, I was successful at bringing my ideas to life. Hearing concepts that originated from ideas within my head was a good feeling. Thinking back on my creations are proud moments for me, especially since I had developed professional skills with such limited access to production equipment.

For many of us today, technology affords us the ability to create music in the comfort of our own homes. You don't necessarily need to be in a recording studio to produce a quality project. When I was starting out, the process of beat making was very time consuming. I spent many hours in the recording studio creating and developing ideas instead of actually recording. It was very costly too. Much of my allowance money or additional financial support from family and friends went directly to paying for studio time. I'll tell you what though: it was my favorite place to be as a teenager. There weren't too many outlets for teenagers my age. If I wasn't playing basketball at a local community center, I was in the studio creating music. I enjoyed every moment of it back then and I still do today.

Being a teenager can be stressful enough, but a youngster with dreams, drive and ambition placed more stress on me. I encountered people that took me for a joke, had little to no faith in me and attempted to take advantage of me. Navigating through the good and bad, or trying to get people to believe in my dreams was exhausting. I was a kid that didn't want to be counted out. I was totally focused and dedicated to my dreams. I was also very serious about my career path even at a young age.

Though I didn't play around much like the other kids because I was so focused on music, when one of my friends brought a basketball to school I couldn't contain myself. Like music I played to the rhythm. I improvised. I shared the spotlight with nasty assists and made pretty sounds as the ball quickly hit the pavement with my sick handling skills.

7

If my family needed to locate me, I was in the studio or in the ball court. To me, learning music production was a game as any sport. In sports there is competition, and rules that determine how to play the game. The competitive effort I showed on the ball court to win was the same drive that I had to win my dream of becoming a music producer.

I continued learning and building my skills with the amateur production equipment that I accrued over the years. The limited features helped shape the production skills I have today. I had to become more creative and find other ways to accomplish my ideas with the lack of professional equipment. The four-track tape recorder was limited because it only allowed for recording on four individual tracks. In order to get the most use out of all four tracks, I would record elements on the first three tracks and then re-record all three tracks onto the last unused track, thereby freeing up three more tracks to re-record on. This process is called "bouncing." I would continue this process until I achieved my desired results. Let me also mention that the quality would deteriorate every time I would repeat the process. It was extra work especially considering today's standards, but it was definitely well worth it to develop my technical and creative skills. Today, the "bouncing" process is obsolete. Digital computer software allows users to have an unlimited amount of tracks to record on without any sound quality lost.

After a while, I had a small makeshift recording set up in my bedroom. I had accumulated a newer version of the Fostex 4-track recorder, Yamaha RY-30 drum machine, Akai S-900 Digital sampler and a Shure Microphone. This was the first legitimate production setup in which I felt like I could make beats at a higher level comparable to beats made by other producers in the game. Equipped with a new setup and feeling confident in my production skills, Caged Fury was ready to take it to the next level. I focused more on production while Cameron and Derek continued to develop as emcees. We were also finishing up high school and it was time for us to go away to college. Fortunately, my school was only two hours away in Connecticut; Cam's school was all the way in Texas. We continued to make songs even though we were living in different states. We booked studio sessions during the holidays and college breaks. Working on limited time, we still managed to create a buzz around Harlem. Lamont "Big L" Coleman heard about us and we eventually began to collaborate. Big L was a rapper from Harlem who was signed to Columbia Records. He was well known for his battling capabilities and his lyrical style. Our association with Big L gave us more exposure and got us closer to our dreams of signing a record deal.

As Caged Fury continued making music, Big L heard one particular song that caught his attention. The song was called "American Dream" which featured Killa Cam (Cameron Giles), Mason "Murda Mase" Betha, Derek "Bloodshed" Armstead, and was produced by yours truly, Darrell "Digga" Branch. Big L wanted to redo "American Dream" adding Herb McGruff and himself onto the track. This was a special achievement because it started my professional production career. Columbia Records on behalf of Big L paid me $1,500.00 for producing the song. This was my first check from the music industry. Up until this point, beat making was all about effort, but now I had confirmation that my dreams in the music industry were coming to fruition.

"American Dream" was recorded and everybody loved the song. After finishing the song, Columbia and Big L didn't do anything with it. At the time of the recording, Cam, Blood and I were the only ones who didn't have a record deal. McGruff was signed to Uptown Records while Mase was signed to Bad Boy Records. We were still making demos and working with our manager George Rowan in attempts to find a deal. We had offers from Blunt Recordings and Freeze Records. We selected the offer from Freeze who had just signed a deal with Jay-Z and Roc-A-Fella Records. Freeze took over where Columbia left off deciding to promote the "American Dream" single. The song received some airplay and won four nights straight on 98.7's "Battle Of The Beats." Caged Fury changed its name to Children Of The Corn, also known as C.O.C. to ride the success of the wave Big L had been creating. Unfortunately, for us, Bad Boy, Columbia and Uptown didn't allow Freeze Records to further promote the single. All three of the labels prohibited their artists from appearing in the video.

Freeze Records paid the three of us weekly per diem while we worked on our album. They provided us with an apartment in Connecticut where I was finishing up my senior year of school. They also provided me with a gem. They gave me a gift as memorable as Christmas when I was eight years old. I was already in Connecticut at the apartment. I had just finished my last class for the day. Cam and our manager George came to the apartment and said, "We got a surprise for you!" Cam handed me a large heavy brown paper bag. He and George were smiling, staring and awaiting my reaction to what was inside the bag. When I looked in the bag, there was an AKAI MPC-3000 Midi Production Center inside. This machine would allow me to create beats within one unit. No need for multiple keyboards, sequencers or drum machines. The MPC series is still one of the most desired pieces of production equipment among many beat makers. At the time, I was shocked and excited; I knew I would be able to take my production to the next level with all the new technological features at my disposal. I finally had a professional music production tool that I desired. I stayed up late for the next few nights reading the manual and testing out all the new features that were now at my musical fingertips.

Cameron, Derek and I started recording demos (song ideas) at my college apartment in Connecticut. We would create music and take the train down to New York City to let the staff at Freeze Records listen. We had only been signed as a recording group for a few months before tragedy struck. In March of 1997 Cameron called the home phone with horrible news, "You didn't hear what happened? Derek is dead! He was killed in a car accident on the Harlem River Drive." I was in total shock. I felt all alone being in my college apartment in Connecticut. I wanted to be in New York City as soon as possible. I wanted answers. I stayed in a state of disbelief for a long time. Derek's death was a reality check in my life. We were on the right path. I thought we were doing the right things; but his death made me realize that none of that mattered. Any one of us, any one of my friends or family could be taken away in the blink of an eye. His death really made me understand the value of life.

After Derek died, Cameron and I didn't go in the studio for weeks. His untimely death made Cameron a solo artist. Meanwhile, our business relationship with Freeze Records had dissolved without explanation. They were no longer paying the rent for our apartment and they stopped giving Cam and I per diem checks. Mase on the other hand was creating a major buzz within the music industry. He was experiencing great success off 112's single "Only You." Mase had previously begun introducing Cameron to music heavyweights; namely Cameron impressed Notorious B.I.G. B.I.G. then introduced Cam to his business partner Lance "Un" Rivera. Unfortunately, tragedy struck again later that month when B.I.G. was also murdered in California. After B.I.G.'s death, Un formed a new label called Untertainment Records and signed Cameron to a deal in early 1997. Killa Cam was now Cam' Ron. Although we had setbacks and tragedies, we continued to push forward and follow our dreams. After graduating from the University of New Haven with a Bachelor of Arts in Music Industry, I was fresh out of college with no job or plan on life.

My opportunity arrived later in 1997 when I was introduced to Un by Cam. I remember being excited about going to the Hit Factory studio. I had a Maxell tape containing about 20 beats. When I walked into the Hit Factory, the first thing I saw were walls aligned with gold and platinum plaques. A big freight elevator took me up to the studio where everyone from Michael Jackson to Bruce Springsteen had recorded in. I walked through the door and introduced myself to everyone. There was dead silence, which made me feel uncomfortable. Un ordered the engineer to show me to the tape player. So, I put my tape in the deck and pressed the play button. Within an instant, the energy in the room changed. My music came through the speakers forcefully, loud and clear. Un smiled and looked around the room in amazement. I knew from that point forward things would change for me. I was standing in the famed Hit Factory, my music blaring from the speakers, everyone nodding their heads to every kick and snare while Cameron cosigned excitedly with "I told you." Less than a week after later, I was offered a deal to become an exclusive producer for Untertainment Records and UN Rivera productions.

Untertainment Records wasn't the only offer I had on the table. Dame Dash, the co-founder of Roc-A-Fella Records offered me a management contract to oversee my career as well. Can you believe that all of a sudden, I had two different offers on the table? For the last five years, Cam, Bloodshed and I were creating music in hopes of landing a recording deal. The opportunity had finally presented itself and the days of mailing demo tapes to record companies with no response were finally over. The days of anxiously awaiting feedback and wondering if, when or where we would land a deal, were finally over. People were ready to listen and things were happening really fast. I quickly moved forward and took the offer presented by Lance Rivera and Untertainment Records. I believed the deal benefit me financially along with providing the best opportunity to be successful.

Jacob York, the president of Untertainment Records suggested that I meet with a few of his attorney friends about possibly representing me during contract negotiations. Was that a good move for me? We'll find out later. The entire legal process was new to me. I didn't know how to hire an attorney, how much he or she should be compensated, or even what he or she would be hired to do. I was honestly learning about things "on the fly." I ended up hiring an attorney who I later found out didn't have my best interest at heart (see "Lawyer Up" on page 32). After about a month of negotiating, I finally agreed to sign my first co-publishing and production deal with Un Rivera Music and Untertainment Records.

So, I'm a professional beat maker, what do I do now? What shouldn't I do? Everything was going so fast at the time, it made me become very defensive and insecure. I was fortunate to go to college and study music and business, but nothing could truly prepare me for the real world experience I encountered. To be honest, once I graduated, I thought I was prepared to handle the treacherous world of the music business but I quickly realized just how naïve I was. When you first break into the music industry, people look at you like fresh meat. They see you as a talent who can create an opportunity for them to share in your success. Everyone wants to be on the winning team. You're the star player now. All type of people want to be your friend or associated with you in some way. Who can you trust? Let's find out as we continue to read *The Beat Game*.

JUMP BALL

What is Hip-Hop Production?

Before you start and dig deep into the world of Hip-Hop production, you need to understand the origins in which the foundation of Hip-Hop was created. Hip-Hop is a cultural movement originally consisting of four elements: emceeing and deejaying (the music), breaking (dancing) and graffiti-writing (artistic expression). Break dancing and graffiti play significant roles in moving the culture forward, however Hip-Hop music and its integral elements have helped spread the culture all around the world.

When you listen to Hip-Hop music today, what are you hearing? What aspects of the genre stand out? Putting aside some of the offensive, misogynistic and profanity laced lyrics, Hip-Hop music is an eclectic art form that infuses many genres of music. It's not just the combination of different genres that make "Hip-Hop music; it's the creative technique and vision of the producer that truly embodies a *Hip-Hop Production*. Hip-Hop production is the act of creating instrumental music that incorporates sampling, scratching, deejaying, beat-boxing and/or live instrumentation to create a "beat" or 'track." Although Hip-Hop music is typically defined as rapping, emceeing, or using the vocal style of speaking with words that rhyme, the background music is what truly defines this genre. There may be other definitions of Hip-Hop, but to say that there is a universal definition for Hip-Hop music or any genre is an understatement. One thing is for sure, the music production of Hip-Hop music is the driving force that creates distinct sounds, and establishes Hip-Hop as a musical genre. For future beat makers, you must understand your historical and future importance in what Hip-Hop is.

In the early seventies, the deejay provided the musical

backdrop for the Emcee by playing records using two turntables. The deejay wouldn't just play any song; they would find a particular song that would have drum grooves, rhythm or instrument solos. Those parts and sections are called a *break* or *break beat*. Originally, the emcee's job was to assist the deejay with crowd participation and to keep the energy alive throughout the festivities in block parties or park gatherings. Today, Hip-Hop producers play a similar role as the deejay, except much of the producer's work is now done in recording studios instead of neighborhood parks.

Introduction of the "Sample Based Producer"

There are a few facts about Hip-Hop production that can't be disputed. Authentic Hip-Hop music consists of an infectious rhythm, elaborate lyrics with the infusion of previous recorded material. According to Dr. Michael Eric Dyson, the first stages in rap record production was characterized by rappers placing their rhythmic, repetitive speech over well-known (mostly R&B) black music hits.[i]

The incorporation of sampling had taken Hip-Hop music to new heights. Therefore, the approach of a Hip-Hop producer is much different then the producer of other genres of music. Most producers create original music using traditional instruments like acoustic drums, guitars, pianos, etc. Sample-based Hip-Hop producers rely on an extensive library of previously recorded music as the source for sounds and instruments. For example, a rock music producer may incorporate drum patterns from a live drummer; while a Hip-Hop producer may sample a drum section from a song (usually played directly from a vinyl record). Then, he or she can manipulate the drum sampler and repeat it.

James Brown, commonly known as "the Godfather of Soul" is probably the most sampled artist of all time. He is recognized as the most influential musician in popular music during the twentieth century. He was instrumental in providing the template for funk, soul and go-go music. The foundation of earlier soul and R&B music was built on major chord progressions with numerous vocal harmonies. James Brown has become a favorite among Hip-Hop producers because his music heavily relied on a rhythmic groove of the drums and bass guitar, with minor emphasis on melody and harmony. Clyde Stubblefield, the drummer who played on many James Brown recordings is one of the most sampled musicians, based on his featured drum performance on the 1970 single "Funky Drummer." James and Clyde influenced a generation of aspiring Hip-Hop producers to develop a music genre built on funk and heavy drums. I had sampled "Funky Drummer" and many other records by Brown during the early stages of my career. Most of the drum and percussion sounds on songs I produced for Cam'Ron such as "357" and "Pimps A Pimp" were borrowed from James Brown recordings.

The deejay used break beats, as the musical backdrop for early Hip-Hop performances. It didn't take long for Hip-Hop producers to use the same formula to create Hip-Hop records. "Rapper's Delight," a 1979 song performed by Hip-Hop group The Sugarhill Gang is considered to be the first recording to popularize Hip-Hop music around the world. The foundation behind the song was built largely on a sample from the 1978 Disco hit song "Good Times" by Chic. The commercial success of the song influenced a generation of Hip-Hop entrepreneurs, musicians and of course, Hip-Hop producers.

In the eighties, Hip-Hop producers pushed their creativity with the evolution of sampling technology. The *digital sampler* was and still is viewed as a musical instrument. Veteran Hip-Hop producers such as Marley Marl, The Bomb Squad, and Rick Rubin were very instrumental in the development of sample-based production. Rick Rubin, the producer and co-founder of Def Jam Recordings was the first to fuse musical elements from Heavy Metal, Rock & Roll and Hip-Hop. His production style led to hits like the 1986 hits "Walk This Way" by Run-DMC and "[You Gotta] Fight For Your Right [To Party!]" by The Beastie Boys.

The mid-nineties brought us some of the most creative producers in Hip-Hop. DJ Premier, J Dilla, Pete Rock and Q-Tip are a few that come to mind when mentioning sampled-based production. Funk, Jazz, Soul, Blues and many other genres continued to influence Hip-Hop music. These producers expanded the way we now think about sampling by using elements like horn riffs, piano melodies, drum rhythms and grooves rather than just basic sample loops. Using these techniques and enhanced sampling capabilities, sample-based music producers pushed the envelope and expanded the genre towards a more original approach.

The Original Composition Producer

During the mid-nineties, Hip-Hop production continued to evolve. Sampling became less prevalent as other emerging technologies and music production became popular. Producers relied less on sampling from older recordings and began to build original compositions combining digital synthesizers and drum machines and real instruments. Legendary producer Dr. Dre pioneered the "West Coast" style by using acoustical instruments and psychotic synthesizer sounds with sampled break beats. Producers such as The Neptunes, Timbaland and Swizz Beatz have embraced technology and changed the approach of overall beat making. Instead of sampling elements like riffs, drums and melodies, these producers were at the forefront of creating beats with original rhythms and melodies.

Other producers explored their creativity and imagination while still maintaining the fundamentals of beat making. Music mogul and producer Sean "Diddy" Combs used a different approach to create some of the biggest hits in Hip-Hop. Instead of sampling directly from an old soul, jazz or funk recordings, Diddy hired beat makers and musicians to recreate specific elements from old recordings to incorporate into his production. This is called an interpolation (see "Sample Replays & Interpolations page 129).

The Roles & Responsibility of a Hip-Hop Producer

A producer plays many roles during the production process. He or she is responsible for supervising and overseeing the entire creative and administrative process of a music project. That means every aspect from the start of an idea to the final mastering mix. Producers organize the studio sessions, guide musicians, hires songwriters, studio engineers or anyone needed to complete the musical project. Most Hip-Hop producers are also beat makers with the skill of Midi programming, sequencing and playing live instruments. Although many use the terms "producer" and "beat maker" interchangeably there is a huge distinction between the two (we'll talk about that later on page 156). Let's look at some of the roles and responsibilities of a Hip-Hop producer:

Pre-Production

A good way for a producer to optimize time during a project is to do pre-production work before the actual recording process begins. Today, many producers have home studios equipped with music production software with recording capabilities to put down song ideas. Pre-production can include anything from administrative duties, concept development, scheduling recording sessions and deciding who will assist you with the project. A producer has to be a good planner; and part of effective planning is preparing in advance. Preparation provides clear direction, builds confidence, and produces the best results.

Artist Communication

One important key to developing a successful project is having good communication skills. As a producer, you will work closely with artists. A producer is the leading voice in a session and able to give direction to all the individuals working on the project. This includes sound engineers, background singers, musicians, writers, and or course the lead artist. During recording sessions, the producer needs to keep everyone focused on the overall goal. The producer also has to give instruction to individuals who need help delivering the overall vision.

Budget Planning

Budget planning is an important and crucial responsibility to the administrative side of a music project. A budget will help a producer keep track of cost and expenses associated with the project. Common expenses include studio cost, hiring musicians, recording engineers and even CD duplication. It is very important for the producer to plan and manage the budget appropriately. Without a good plan, a recording project budget can reach its limit very quickly which could limit or halt the production process.

Final Project

The final project is the end result of the entire production process including but not limited to, pre-production, communication and budgeting. Always remember, the main goal of the producer is to bring the best performances out of the artist and musicians working on the project. A producer monitors all aspects of the production process, which includes beat making, developing song ideas, writing, programming, recording, mixing and mastering. Producers are usually judged based on his or her effectiveness at providing leadership, which produces high quality results during a project.

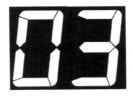

The Dream Team

"The key players that will help you along the path of success."

In 1985, wrestlers Brutus Beefcake and Greg Valentine of the World Wrestling Federation (now known as WWE) joined forces as a tag team at the height of their success. The United States assembled a basketball team with some of the best NBA players such as Michael Jordan, Magic Johnson and Larry Bird to compete in the 1992 World Olympics. OJ Simpson hired a high-profile team of attorneys to defend him in his 1995 murder case. What do these teams have in common? All of these teams were called "The Dream Team." They were assembled with either top athletes or the best individuals capable of working together to achieve success and to secure a win.

As the producer and leader of your own business, you will quickly realize how challenging and time-consuming the work can be. To alleviate the workload of your responsibilities is why you need to surround yourself with a team of individuals who can effectively manage the areas you lack expertise in. Most musical Dream Teams should consist of four members: An *attorney, manager, accountant* and close *friend*. These members are the key players that will help you along the path of success. They should share your entrepreneurial drive and vision to increase business opportunities.

Selecting members of your Dream Team will take serious thought and consideration. They will help guide your future actions and decision-making throughout your career. If you have a close friend who has a level head and isn't close to the business, try getting their honest opinion on situations or issues concerning your career. He or she may have good insight on what type of members should be on the team. A close friend should also be a good judge of character.

Now, this doesn't mean you should bring in four random people willing to do the job and desire to become a member of your Dream Team. You will be the leader of this team and responsible from guiding them in the right direction. Contrary to popular belief, people won't work unless they have a good reason to so you will need to make sure prospective members share the same vision (we will go more in detail later).

Success, fame and money are factors that can influence and encourage prospective members to want to join your team. Knowing that you can be a success adds incentive and motivation for members to perform. After all, everyone wants to be a part of a winning team whether they are sitting on the bench as a reserve, or actually in the game contributing.

As the leader of your team, you need to build a great rapport with each member of the team so that they will do the best job possible. "You need people who truly believe in your gift and are just as excited about your career as you are," says producer and YouTube sensation Bonnie Mayfield. A great manager will be dedicated to you and prepared to go out and fight their way in every door for you. When the finances start to roll in, you will definitely need an accountant to help you with budgets, bills and to get your taxes in order.

Not all Dream Team members need to be previously trained, educated professionals. Training and education are never negative things; but there are other factors that may produce a more positive or goal-oriented outcome. Family members are possibly way closer to you than business professionals that are strangers. You may find them more suitable to handle different aspects of your career. Look at how many mother/managers (also called "momagers") we have had, or we have, in the music industry today. They used to be looked at like nuisances in comparison to typical industry managers. Seasoned professionals wanted the parents to step aside and let them handle things. Now, they are more common, and forces to be reckoned with.

Your Dream Team can be a network of people who provide unconventional resources to you. Production and DJ trio Cookin' Soul are able to split many responsibilities amongst themselves enabling them to build a larger network. They say that they are their "own Dream Team in reality." They dedicate more time to whatever is needed at a specific time. Taking on the roles of their Dream Team has helped them build relationships with some of the most important DJs in the game, like DJ Drama, DJ Whoo Kid and Don Cannon. They have also built friendships with the most important blogs like 2dopeboyz.com, Nahright.com and Thisis50.com.[ii]

During the recruiting process for prospective members, choose the best individuals that have you your best interest at heart. These individuals should share your values and maintain a high sense of integrity. Be prepared to manage a group of individuals with various skill sets and personalities.

Management (The Career Planner)

"A good manager should have great communication skills, strong relationships, a good ear and a ton of patience."

I know what you're thinking. *I have a whole batch of hot beats but I'm unable to get them to artists at the record label because I don't have the "connections."* You think If you had a manager, your problems would be solved right? Contrary to popular belief, a manager is not responsible for *shopping your beats* or getting you a placement on an album. A manager's main focus should be your **professional career.** " You know, some people think of a manager as someone who is supposed to go out and get them work and that's absolutely false. That's a pro-active manager. Managers are supposed to manage all the stuff that's going on all around you to make sure it's in organizational mode," says producer/DJ Don Cannon.[iii] Production manager, Sarah J has a different view. "The main two things I make sure I'm doing for my clients each day are getting them work and exposure! It's so important for producers to market themselves just like artists these days."[iv]

Don Cannon knows that the role of his managers is to organize and simplify his life. In today's industry, these roles are ever expanding. Managers, especially newer ones to the game may take on more tasks than ever before. The result is a heavier workload with other job titles possibly phasing out. Yandy Smith, star of the reality show, Love & Hip Hop is an example of this type of new age manager. As the ex-manager of rapper Jim Jones, Yandy handled matters for him, which was outside of the professional realm.[v] In a 2011 radio interview, she mentioned that some of her duties included managing her client's personal issues as well as his business affairs. For example, when Jim got arrested for driving with a suspended license, Yandy was the one who went to the police precinct to bail him out with her own money. In general, the role of a manager is to organize and simplify an artist's life. However, the current economy and ever changing industry has encouraged downsizing and multitasking. Some "new style" managers would rather be employed; taking on extra tasks no matter how stressful or daunting.

We commonly leave out the word "personal" when referring to the management job title, but the word is very significant and shouldn't be removed. We have all been brainwashed to believe that business should never be personal. In this industry, it's definitely PERSONAL! A manager is a spokesperson and a reflection of you. There are times when some executives won't meet with you unless you have a manager. Executive's requisites of meeting with your manager signify the importance of a manager's role in securing you business advantages. You want a person who possesses all the skills needed to help you have a successful career. A great manager should be well educated in publishing, record labels, production, publicist, recording engineers, advertising, film and any other industry field you choose to incorporate into your career plan. Of course, managers have additional responsibilities such as:

1. Being the middle person between you and the industry world.
2. Helping you with business and creative decisions.
3. Promoting you to everyone.
4. Creating a marketing campaign to maximize your potential.
5. Driving your vision and creating a platform for your future ventures.

As the leader of your Dream Team, your manager will ultimately be responsible for making sure everyone is working together because they are all working with you. But most importantly, they are working for you!

A personal manager is responsible for guiding your professional career and leading your Dream Team. Good managers usually can get people working together to accomplish the overall goal of success for its clients. If you have members of your team who aren't communicating with each other, you can't expect positive results. Managers are like basketball coaches. Their main job is making sure each player is performing to their best ability while working together as a team. Just like a basketball team who may have one or two star players, the coach has to make sure all the players follow the game plan strategies. The other members of your team including your attorney, business manager and personal assistant (when you when you become real successful) should work closely with your manager.

Tony Perez of Relentless Management has represented some of the top songwriters and producers in the game such as Sean Garrett, The Heatmakerz, Needlz, Sean C & LV, Midi Mafia and I, to name a few. He believes an effective manager needs to remain focused in four areas. "A good manager should have great communication skills, strong relationships, a good ear and a ton of patience for BS."[vi]

Quick scenario: *An A&R representative from Roc Nation is about to start working on the new Jay Z project. He or she has a list of contacts, which includes beat makers, producers, colleagues and managers.*

Should you or your manager be on the A&R's radar? Who will the A&R want to reach out to you to hear your music?

Your manager should be on that list of course. If he or she isn't on the list, your manager needs to do everything in their power to initiate contact and communication with the A&R. It's important that your manager uses the correct approach. If he or she sends an email or calls with an arrogant attitude, an A&R representative will be less receptive to continue communication.

Management Deals

The management deal is the first type of business agreement most beat makers will come across. As I began to meet people and showcase my work, I would stumble upon people who would offer to help get my music exposed in various ways. What I quickly discovered was that the help they were offering was a proposition in the form of a *management deal*. When someone offers to pitch your music in exchange for money, you are negotiating a management deal. Another form of a management deal is if an individual is given permission to negotiate terms of a deal on your behalf. The role of the manager comes with a broad range of duties and responsibilities. This is why understanding the essential deal points are necessary to constructing the best possible management deal.

A management deal is a written and/or verbal agreement between you (the beat maker) and an individual or management company allowing the exclusive right to exploit your work and represent you as a music producer. Typical management deals are written agreements that focus on four key areas (also referred to as "clauses"): *Commission, Term, Compensation* and *Power Of Attorney*. Here is a description of each clause in detail:

Commission

The industry standard for a manager's commission can range anywhere between 15 to 20% - sometimes even a higher percentage of your gross earnings. If the commission is 20% that means that 20 cents from every dollar you earn is immediately deducted for their compensation. Now, of course it is possible to negotiate with a manager because ANY DEAL IS NEGOTIABLE! Keep in mind: if you're just starting out, the odds of you negotiating anything other than a standard deal are slim to none without some type of leverage. It all depends on your *bargaining power* and your current situation. Today that means how in-demand you are and what type of buzz you are generating. A manager may agree to a lower percentage in exchange for a longer-term provision in the contract (we'll talk about this in a minute). The point is, you have some negotiating room to make sure that all parties are happy, especially you of course.

Terms

The terms of the agreement is important to all parties involved. It should be clear that the agreement should be for a period starting on a specific date and continuing until the established end date set. Although a long-term deal might be appealing, I would recommend that you shorten the deal to no more than one year with an *option to extend* it. This will help give you time to assess the manager's performance and to evaluate if the relationship is moving in the right direction. The artist needs time to determine how effective the manager is and will be. Conversations, meetings and other forms of communication are all needed but the "proof is in the pudding:" the actual work being done.

Compensation

Even when the term of the agreement reaches the ending period, it doesn't necessarily mean you stop paying commission fees to your manager. Under this provision, the manager gets paid on earnings generated after the term as a result of "contracts entered into or substantially negotiated during the term." That means that the manager will continue to be paid a commission on all deals generated under the original agreement. *Beware of any language that suggests, "Post term commissions.* I've heard of ex-managers earning part of a producer's income without being connected to music just because of this clause.

Power of Attorney

A *Power of Attorney clause* gives your manager the power to sign and approve any types of contracts on your behalf. It can also give them the authority to receive payments and cash your checks. Essentially, giving your manager the power of attorney also gives him or her the ability to sell your music without your approval. At no point should you give anyone the power to sign or enter into an agreement on your behalf without your approval. There may be special circumstances when you will need to give your manager the permission to act on your behave. For example, you may be physically unable to sign important documents because you are in another country. In this case, it may be feasible for him or her to gain approval and sign the documents on your behalf. Allowing power of attorney should only happen on a case-by-case basis. Never, and I mean *never give your manager full Power of Attorney authority* during the entire duration of your management agreement.

Creative Deals

Not all management deals are done on such a formal basis. I've done deals on a handshake with the understanding that commission would be paid only on income generated by the manager. Informal strategies keep deals simple and ensure that your manager has an incentive to work hard. Don Cannon has structured a similar management deal too. "My managers and I are more like partners. If they happen to bring in some work for me, of course they are going to eat off that situation. But if I create the situation, that's killing the deer and bringing it back home. The percentage of what they [receive] would be different," Cannon explains.[iii] In this structure, Don Cannon benefits significantly because he pays his management team their full percentage only on work generated and negotiated by the management team themselves. Creative deals allow beat makers to structure management commission fees based on their needs. Once you reach a certain level of success, your manager will be less responsible for soliciting work on your behalf.

Management Players

An NBA General Manager with the number one draft pick has a job to choose the best available player who will help the team win. While evaluating players, the GM will look for certain skill levels in key areas like ball handling, shooting, intelligence and leadership. There may be 10 different players who excel in those areas. So how does a GM choose the right player? The GM needs to do some research and consider additional factors to make a final decision. Researching and analyzing is exactly what you will need to do when choosing a manager. Of course, your manager should meet the basic qualifications, but there are also other factors that need to be considered. Over the course of my career, I've noticed a trend in the styles and business structures of managers. The following categories should give you an idea of what to expect.

The "CEO" Manager

A management firm is structured like a typical corporation and usually maintains a positive reputation. It represents "A-List" clientele and is also well connected with the "who's-who" of the music industry. A "CEO" manager usually holds a leadership position at a management firm. As a client, you are assigned a *point person* or mini manager. CEO managers usually limit contact with their clients and mainly focuses on dedicating time to their high earning clients. At first glance, being part of a *"major management team"* may sound quite appealing to the aspiring beat maker. However there are major obstacles to overcome within this structure. Even if a "CEO Manager" decides to take you on as a client, as a beat maker, you will find yourself competing against fellow clients for the attention of management. On the positive side, this structure may have huge benefits for the producer looking to be associated with "A-List" clientele. You must evaluate if this type of structure will benefit you at different stages in your career.

The "Groupie" Manager

There are some managers with a *limited amount of morals* who stoop to any level to gain exposure, attention and/or attain some amounts of success. Their clients are usually individuals who are uneducated on the business and easily influenced. The "groupie" manager will use any tactic to gain a relationship with an influential executive. Some "groupie" managers are working for you even when you don't know it. If they can get there hands on your music, they may set up meetings as if they represent you as a client. I've heard of "groupie" managers setting up meetings to play beats made by 20 different producers without consent. Even though he or she may not be a representative hired by you, he or she can create a bad image of you simply by the way he or she handles your affairs. You should absolutely *stay away from the "groupie" managers and their management style* because it could damage your reputation within the industry beyond repair.

The "Hey Mon" manager

"Hey Mon" is a reference that comes from a skit on Fox network's sketch comedy program "In Living Color" (1990-1994). The skit was based on a Jamaican family who had an outrageous amount of jobs to support themselves in America. "Hey Mon" managers are not focused on their management responsibilities 100% of the time. They usually have their hands in different areas of the industry. For instance, they may be working at promotion, A&R along with managing. They may even hold a full-time job totally independent of their management duties. You can assess if this type of part time management style is acceptable to you based upon your needs and level of success.

28

The "True Believer" Manager

There are individuals who truly believe in their clients' skills and abilities. These managers will *ride or die* for you. They sing your praises and will stand beside you as your number one fan. The amount of hours invested in you and your career may be limitless. Everybody wants or needs a manager like this at some point in his or her career. In this game it's important to have a support system as well as people who believe in your work as much as you do. These managers may lack some of the traditional management skills necessary initially, but their hard work can make up for it all. No matter what management style you prefer, all managers should encompass "true believer" manager characteristics.

What Managers Need From You

If your manager is doing his or her job, they will have high expectations for you. They will expect you to hold up your end of the deal by improving your skills, staying on task and promoting yourself along with what they do. As a client, you need to do everything in your power to make your manager's job easy. Making their job easier entails giving them a quality product, adhering to deadlines and maintaining your professional standard. The last thing a manager wants to do is waste time, especially because of a client's unprofessionalism and lack of production. "I like to work with people who are consistent and can bring that new sound to the game; a producer who is motivated and can keep up with my work ethic!" says Sarah J.[iv]

D.I.Y. Management

D.I.Y. (Do it Yourself) management is not such a difficult task if you have the time and resources. Actually, self-management is a responsibility that all aspiring producers will have to take on during the early stages of their careers. A common question from beat makers is: *how do I find a manager?* My response is: ***stop looking and get out there and find your own work!*** When your career takes off and you build a demand for your work, a professional manager will most likely try to recruit you. They are always looking for talent but you may not always need or desire professional management. After all, management is all about responsibility, planning and organization. If you are a responsible person, you should be able handle your own scheduling, appointments, networking, etc.

"Some people have a manager; I have a school calendar with all the shaded areas for the days off. I like having my business right in front of me, I like being able to do everything" says producer Prince Paul.

Every beat maker should have on his or her personal calendars online and offline that are used for organizing their schedules and appointments. (See illustration 1 below.)

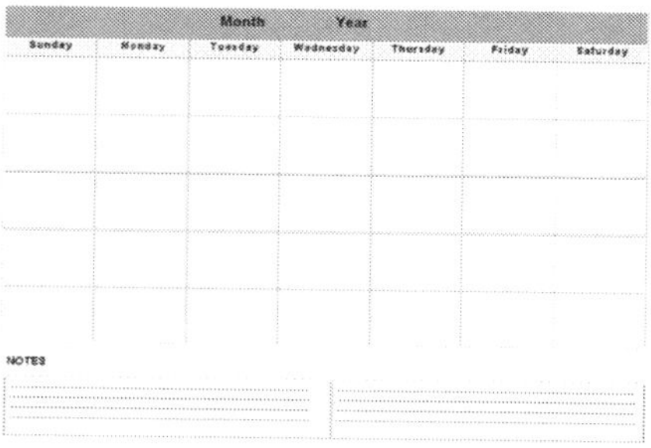

Illustration 1.

Now, just because you act as your own manager doesn't mean you won't need help from others. You should take advantage of the resources around you like good friends or family. If you have difficulty planning out your schedule, have someone close to you do it for you. Almost every personal computer or mobile device has a calendar or planner to guide your daily life. While a daily planner will help with scheduling, you will also need to be *disciplined*, have good negotiation skills, determination and patience (we'll talk about that in part II).

"I don't give everybody the responsibility to the point where I can cry about them not doing what they are supposed to do. I do everything myself. Then delegate out specific things. That way I know everything will run smoothly," Don Cannon advises.[iii]

Hiring A Manager

Managers should be hired to help you advance, simplify, organize and maintain your career. This doesn't mean you should hand over all responsibility to them either. You are totally responsible for yourself, your creations and what your manager does on your behalf. Always keep in mind that a manager works for you and not the other way around. You should make all the final decisions after consulting with your manager and other people you trust.

The manager you select will be important to your career, your earnings and future earning potential. With that in mind, hire a manager you feel comfortable with and that you believe is trustworthy. Make sure he or she is willing to commit the time needed to develop and maintain your career. Ideally, you will need a powerful, well-connected and respected person. If that isn't readily available, look for a dedicated, heavy in common sense, hard working, persistent, "won't take no for an answer" candidate. As an aspiring producer, you should always try to find a manager and team members who display hustle, determination, good communication skills and an overall interest in getting the job done. These positive attributes can help a manager develop the power and respect within the industry in due time.

If you decide to hire a manager and you can't find someone you can trust, the alternative must be to manage oneself. Your business is just as personal to you as your family. If you take your work seriously and your music creations are your babies, then you must hire a manager that you have full faith and one hundred percent trust in. Expecting these ideals might sound generic and maybe even unrealistic but it's the best foundation for hiring a manager outside of taking on the responsibility yourself. Trust, determination and overall common sense may compensate for the lack of experience in the management field in most cases.

Lawyer Up "The Legal Player"

"I try my best to reach all of my clients by obtaining a level of trust, understanding and respect so that we have an open and free flowing level of communication."

Who is the first person a criminal suspect wants to talk to when they get into trouble? Who is the first person you need to talk to when you believe you have been treated unfairly? Who can interpret the law and explain legal concepts clearly so that you can easily understand? The first person that comes to mind is an attorney or lawyer. I personally have a cousin who is a lawyer. Any time something happens in my family, even the smallest of dilemmas, we want to get him on the phone. My wife has a best friend who is an attorney as well; my wife definitely does not hesitate to drop a scenario or two by her attorney friend for some free and respected legal advice. But before you start asking yourself, *aren't a lawyer and an attorney the same thing?* Let me answer you: technically, there is a difference. An ***attorney*** is a professional qualified to represent a client. Meaning, an attorney *doesn't have to be trained in the field of law.* An attorney can hold the "power of attorney," therefore can legally handle business and execute documents on your behalf. A ***lawyer*** is a person *trained in the field of law* and provides advice on legal matters.[vii] Because a lawyer can also represent their client, the title "attorney" and "lawyer" are sometimes used interchangeably. The difference between an attorney and lawyer is a very important distinction that can largely be overlooked, especially if you're not careful with choosing the right person to represent you.

All attorneys should be licensed to practice law. Just because someone "represents" you, even in good faith, it doesn't mean they are trained in the field of law well enough to provide the best advice for your situation.

While establishing a positive relationship with every member of your team is important, building a strong foundation with your attorney is highly critical. Depending on your business structure and career plan, your attorney could play the second most important role on your Dream Team. Your personal manager may handle your day-to-day concerns and issues, but an effective attorney can help alleviate long-term concerns by structuring deals and agreements in your favor. Not only can the attorney construct deals in your favor but also create incentives that add revenue for things you may have never considered, or understood, as possible sources of income. The role of attorneys are much more than just looking over contracts and advising their clients. Unlike other members of your Dream Team, attorneys will be involved in all areas associated with your production career, even on down to negotiating your management contact. Recording deals, publishing deals, performance rights deals and management deals are all agreements that will come across your attorney's desk throughout your career. The manager might find the deals, but the lawyer makes them lucrative, ensures you're treated fairly, and secures your future by making the appropriate amendments and mark-ups on the agreements listed above.

Before you get on the Internet to start your "Google" search of entertainment lawyers and attorneys, there are a few precautions you should take into consideration previous to choosing one. *All attorneys and lawyers are not created equal!* Just because a person is able to pass the state bar examination, or is licensed to practice law does not make them qualified, skilled or trustworthy. The biggest misconception about attorneys and other licensed professionals is that they posses competent traits. We commonly assume that professionals who have reached certain levels of education can be entrusted in high confidence. All professional representatives should be seen on a level playing field until proven dependent.

You can't assume an attorney who represents a film client can give you advice on the best publishing deal. A criminal attorney or family law attorney probably won't be well versed in music production contracts or publishing deals. Believe it or not, some attorneys lack common sense and basic business knowledge. Ideally, you want the attorney you choose to have superior knowledge about production, publishing, management and all other areas of music.

Key Factors when Choosing a Lawyer

When looking to retain *legal counsel* (another fancy word for lawyer or attorney), make sure you look into their reputation, education, and experience.

Reputation

You should find out as much information about the prospective attorney's reputation. Find out if the attorney has already represented any successful artist, managers, or record labels. With outstanding work and extensive knowledge lawyers gain credibility and lasting reputations. You can make wise and informed decisions if you first speak to persons who have previously been represented by potential lawyers. Having these conversations can give you inside information on personality, business ethics and other information on how hard a lawyer has worked for them. In this age of the Internet, it's easy for anyone, including lawyers to falsify their work history and resumes by making websites look way glamorous or by embellishing their clientele lists. First hand accounts are the best sources of information.

Education

A prospective attorney should be in good standing at his or her State Bar. Your attorney in question should ideally practice *entertainment law* or *contract law*. He or she should preferably, be involved in the music industry. They should also be highly experienced in the fields of: *publishing, copyrights, recording, performance and foreign rights*. Music industry contracts, like most, are very particular and very intense; the slightest number being off, even by a penny, could drastically decrease your current and future earnings. Making sure you get every penny you earn should not be taken lightly, and neither should the education of your attorney.

Ten years ago there weren't any 360 deals[1]. Now all the record labels are interested in signing new artist to these kinds of deals. If a lawyer doesn't continue to educate oneself on all the latest twist and turns in relation to music deals, the client is sure to suffer and at risk of losing out on potentially lucrative opportunities.

Experience

A good attorney should have a great track record and an impressive resume suited to your needs. Attorneys fresh on the industry scene, with limited experience will also be capable of reviewing contracts to determine if they are fair or not. Since they are rookies, they are most likely available at cheaper rates than veteran attorneys.

Attorneys with experience may charge more, but the advantages could be worth it. Veteran attorneys establish a level playing field in the industry. Labels may know seasoned and competent industry attorneys simply by name recognition, and understand right from the door that they won't be able to play games with your legal counsel. Experienced attorneys can evaluate contracts quickly, therefore saving you money. They know what to ask for and when; which helps you by getting the best deals. They know what to demand in a contract, which protects you from becoming bound to a contract unfairly, and makes it easier for future changes and earning potential.

A new attorney may not be well versed on intricate details or incentives that can be requested simply because of a of lack experience on the matter. During your search for an attorney, I recommend that you find an individual with experience in handling matters relevant to Hip-Hop music. An attorney who specializes in matters relevant to Rock-N-Roll music may find it challenging to understand Hip-Hop concepts and common procedures.

---

[1] A 360 deal is a contract that allows the record label to receive a percentage of the earnings from all of an artist's activities rather than just earning from record sales. Record labels earn a percentage of money made from concert revenue, merchandise sales, endorsements deals, and ringtones.

What An Attorney Should Do For You

We expect attorneys to be everything close to miracle workers. We expect them to have super powers and make the impossible happen without having clear expectations. I agree a hundred percent with Producer Nottz who said, "The best thing an attorney can do for me is make sure my rights are protected."[viii] Your attorney should always protect you from anything that could be harmful to your pockets and career. In being a great legal defender, your lawyer must be wise, willing to educate him or herself while being an excellent communicator. A good lawyer must be able and prepared to explain contract details, strategies and the rights of his or her clients. Most agreements are based on producers giving exclusive rights to record labels, publishers, distributors, etc. Attorneys need to do two things: *educate* and *seal the deal*.

Attorney Matt Middleton is also in support of educating his clients:

> The most important thing I would say is to educate them as much as possible about the copyright laws and all of the changes that are being debated due to the changes in technology and how music is consumed so that they can make informed decisions during the creative process and on the business side.[ix]

Your attorney should be able to read over an agreement and explain it to you in detail. Not all attorneys see the importance in educating their clients. There are some attorneys who believe less communication with their clients is for the better. When referring to the act of reviewing and editing a proposed contract agreement, producers have experienced that some attorneys will make decisions and do mark-ups, but not explain anything.[x] If your attorney has an issue doing so, you need to find a different attorney *fast*.

Turnaround time is an important factor when choosing an attorney. We live in an era where opportunities come quickly and can disappear just as fast. You want to be able to speak with your attorney without going on a "callback list." You need to be able to make an appointment and get counseling within a reasonable period of time.

Contracts are only offered within a given time frame or the deal on the table may expire. Find an attorney who understands your business needs and time constraints. Producer !llmind said it best when he told me, "The best thing an attorney can do for you is accomplish the task at hand in a fair and timely fashion."[xi]

What An Attorney *Should Not* Do For You

We listen to attorneys for their *professional* opinions. We expect them to provide us with the information to make wise and informed decisions.

Under no circumstance should an attorney force or pressure you into making a decision. If you don't agree with or understand a decision after a consultation, you may need to re-evaluate your relationship with your attorney. People that work for you may forget that final outcomes are ultimately yours to deal with alone. Financial loss or financial gains affect you. Attorneys will be able to bill you and get paid regardless of you losing money off of a deal they brokered or not. Attorneys do not lose based on your downfall, but when you win, they share in your success.

Dealing with a lawyer could be like a point guard throwing an "alley-oop" pass to you for the slam-dunk. Both players share the wealth in a successful basketball play; you get credit for the score and the point guard gets credit for the assist. However, if you miss the dunk, the point guard will still get praise for "the good look," while you get the blame for missing the easy score. It's always a win-win for the attorney, so consider your options when you need to make a move forward, pull back or take a time-out to thoroughly think a big decision through.

Don't be rushed into making an important decision. Of course, an attorney should advise you to make an informed decision but the final word should always be yours. While watching political coverage during the 2008 presidential election, MSNBC news commentator, Chris Matthews said something that made a lot of sense that applies in this situation. He said, "I don't question motive. It's the worst thing you can do in journalism is try to figure out motive. There's no way to determine it."[xii] His advice is true, and expresses the main reason why you should make your own decisions. Unfortunately, even the most ethical attorneys can sometimes have ulterior motives to complete a deal.

Although your attorney is responsible for drafting agreements and negotiating deals, you should play an active role during negotiations to develop a winning strategy. You want to position yourself in the negotiations to make the best decision. Don't rely on your attorney to take it upon him or herself to form a strategy without communicating with you. Veteran producer Mr. Devine cautions against lawyers who will do mark-ups without explaining anything to their clients.[xiii] Don't assume that all attorneys have good negotiating skills and bargaining power. A good practice is to ask questions about contract mark-ups and not to move forward until every single one is explained to you. Don't assume: don't say things like "this *must mean*," or "this *has to be talking about*." Not being able to say exactly what is meant or being said means you are unsure, and "guess work" doesn't cut it when your talking contracts and signing your name to a deal. Make the lawyer explain each and every detail because there isn't any turning back after signing on the dotted line. It doesn't matter whether you understand what was requested or required upon signing the documents, you will be on the hook to deliver.

Try and find an attorney who sits on speaking panels, music boards and consistently aware on new industry trends. As we discussed earlier, attorneys who educate and communicate with their clients are able to advise more effectively. But if you're not careful, your attorney can give you the wrong advice, which could affect your career in the long term. Hopefully they will be knowledgeable about the latest deals and trends.

Legendary Hip-Hop producer Buckwild was probably given the worse advice any attorney could offer. When he first started, he had an attorney tell him to "just take the money so you can get paid."[xiv] The attorney totally disregarded all the conditions within the proposed deal just so his client could secure the deal. Once the deal was secure, the attorney received a ***commission*** (see "Fees & Compensation" on page 47). The attorney's recommendation was formed by his own personal motivation of financial gain. An attorney should never encourage or persuade its client to accept a deal without explaining what the future consequences might be. It is unethical for any attorney to put his or her own financial interest ahead of his or her client's line of business. Hiring an unethical and unscrupulous attorney can get you in all kinds of trouble if you're not careful.

When an Attorney's Advice Goes Wrong

Your attorney plays a role, which can be compared to the point guard position in the sport of basketball. Attorneys are responsible for setting up plays and carrying out the strategy to put you (his or her client) in the best position to score. But just like in basketball, everything doesn't always go according to plan when the game is played. Your point guard - your attorney, may not be a team player. Here are two examples of how an attorney's advice can possibly damage your career beyond repair.

Example#1: WWE Buyout Deal

Jake One, producer for Hip-Hop artists such as 50 Cent, Freeway and Rick Ross, made a terrible decision based on advice given to him by his attorney. His attorney told him to accept a buyout from the WWE for the Jon Cena album. "He was telling me to accept the deal because they weren't going to use my song unless I accepted a total buyout."[xv] A *buyout* is when a producer agrees to transfer all of his or her rights in a master recording in exchange for a one-time payment. Jake One continues, "He didn't think we could get them to give me any part of the publishing share either. Considering that Cena's theme song has played millions of times over the past 10 years it was a terrible idea. Even if I received 5% of the publishing income, I would have came up." After accepting a one-time payment, Jake One forfeited all of his potential future earnings. Traditional production deals are usually structured so that the producer receives a "royalty" each time his or her original work is performed. Under traditional deals, you can potentially earn more money and maintain a revenue stream over the long term.

Keep in mind: all buyout deals aren't necessarily bad. Jake One felt that he could've potentially made more money without the deal, but didn't mention the amount of money he received to complete the buyout deal. Let's just assume that Jake One received a payment between $10,000 and $100,000; such large sums of money may be considered to be a great buyout deal to most people.

In the long run, the deal in the WWE scenario could have been more lucrative. The possibility of the "Jon Cena" theme being exploited in various ways (performed on T.V., radio, commercials, etc.) could generate substantially more revenue than the buyout deal by issuing individual licenses for each use.

Example#2: Time on My Side Deal

I produced five songs for an artist signed to a major label (artist, label and attorney shall remain nameless for sensitivity reasons). The artist and label were very excited about the project and were in a hurry to negotiate and finalize a deal. After about a week, my attorney received the first draft of the production agreement between the artist and I (see "Production Deals" on page 82). To my surprise, the written agreement contained conditions and deal points I couldn't possibly agree to. The amount of my production fee was rejected. Considering the fact that my attorney had already discussed my production fee with the artist's attorney, I found it odd that I was offered *half* the amount I initially quoted. It's not uncommon for opposing attorneys to resort to these type of negotiation tactics. The goal is to make all deal points negotiable, no matter what may have been discussed previously.

With negotiation being an integral part of the legal process, I assumed that my attorney would have my best interest in mind but I quickly realized that I was wrong. After ironing out most of the deal points, my production fee was still an unresolved issue. My attorney suggested that I think about accepting a lower fee to speed-up the legal process, and not jeopardize the entire deal. After thinking it over for about two weeks, I accepted the deal taking 20% less than the original production fee quoted. I was motivated to accept the deal because I knew my initial quote was actually 25% more then I anticipated receiving anyway. *I was satisfied in the end.* On the other hand, my attorney wanted to close the deal to quickly get his cut. He did not want to endure the negotiation process any longer. Yet because I took the time to evaluate the deal, I made sure I was getting the best deal. An attorney won't wager their whole business operation on a single deal.

These types of situations and scenarios are not uncommon, particularly for new producers who lack experience in these matters. It is imperative that you work with an attorney who can educate you, explain your options in detail and assist you with developing a strategic plan for negotiation purposes. Once you have evaluated your options and resolved any issues with the deal, you should feel at ease making an informed decision.

Cookies & Milk

Some producers are much more proactive; they make the proper adjustments to satisfy their legal needs based on lessons learned from difficult experiences. Producer Don Cannon has a production coordination team called "Cookies & Milk."[xvi] The team also represents other producers such as Lil Jon, DJ Toomp and Shawty Red. With great working relationships with the administration departments at most of the major record labels and publishing companies, Cookies & Milk cut down the legal workload considerably. Don Cannon attributes Cookies & Milk's success by doing all the paperwork, which made it easier for the attorneys to focus on contracts and deal proposals. Time plays an important factor in all business transactions and as a client of a high profile attorney, you may need to step in and facilitate the legal process. Using strategies Cookies & Milk's production coordination team practices cuts down on precious time, which benefits the producer's affairs.

Attorney Personality Styles & Traits

During your search for legal counsel, you will find that the most challenging part about your search is finding an attorney who has a good reputation, respected credentials and an effective communication style acceptable to help guide your career. An attorney's style consists of a combination of personality traits: integrity, ethics and overall approach within the entertainment industry. There are thousands of qualified attorneys available but you need to choose an effective attorney capable of communicating with you and people within the industry.

An experienced attorney is able to use "clout" within the industry to make things happen. Like in any business field, people tend to feel more comfortable working with people they know. This is why it is important for an attorney to build healthy working relationships and good lines of communication with individuals. Matt Middleton, an attorney from Simon, Eisenberg & Baum LLP has represented Grammy Award winning songwriters and multi-platinum selling recording artists. He gave me his take on attorney styles. "I would say a particular attorney's style plays a role in whether or not they are successful in dealing with any client, not just 'Hip- Hop' clients," Middleton said.[xvii] Not all attorneys communicate in the same way and some use a style and approach that may be unconventional. The overall goal is to be effective for clients. "I try my best to reach all of my clients by obtaining a level of trust, understanding and respect so that we have an open and free flowing level of communication" according to Middleton.

During my own search to hire an attorney, I discovered an intriguing theme, which recurred within the information I gathered. I noticed that based on specific personality traits and styles, attorneys can be grouped into categories. The categories have expanded based on my continued experience, communication and interaction with various attorneys. My hope is to bring attention to the importance of evaluating personality traits and styles during the search process to find the right attorney for you. I'm sure you will find this guide helpful during your attorney search.

The five categories of personality and traits I advise to take caution when considering hiring attorneys are: the "Hollywood" attorney, the "Just to Get a Rep" attorney, the "Big Thinker" attorney, the "Homeboy" attorney, and the "Power Broker" attorney. Here's a brief description of each type you may come across during your search.

The "Hollywood" Attorney

Have you ever heard the quote "you gotta fake it, until you make it?" Well, that's how "Hollywood" attorney conduct it's business. His or her ultimate goal is to create the illusion that their name or the firms name says and does it all. *Perception* is a powerful tool used in efforts to appear to be something that's not (we'll dive deep into this later).

Say you walk into a crowded restaurant for the first time around 7:30 during the evening time. Everyone appears to be having fun. The waitresses are moving fast to serve their guests, and the food smells delicious. After about 5 minutes, you might come to the conclusion that *this must be a great restaurant.*

What if you find out that the entire restaurant of guests who arrived before 7:00PM was given a free meal?

Do you feel the same way now?

Have you ever wondered why lines can be so long when you go out "clubbing?" Most clubs hold a line outside so that when prospective club goers pass by, they will see people waiting to get inside. This environment creates anticipation and a need to get in the line. After all, *these people must be waiting for the excitement of what's inside.* But how do you feel when you get inside and the dance floor is empty and people are sitting around?

These are common tactics for clubs and restaurants to effect your perception, to make people want in, and hopefully they'll stay once they finally get inside.

In both examples, the businesses formulated a plan, which created an atmosphere similar to what would be expected in Hollywood: a glamorous experience. Creating an attractive perception is exactly what Hollywood attorneys do. They trick their current and prospective clients by creating situations that make the lawyer appear to have substantial credit; when in actuality they may not be very helpful.

There are tricks to every trade; "Hollywood" Attorneys

recognize and exploit the power of perception. One of their tricks includes making the client wait. In an attempt to appear busy, some attorneys won't take phone calls or meetings right away. A super plush office with all the trimmings including excess staff provides you with the Hollywood optics. I have met attorneys with very little clientele but they had three personal assistants, one business manager, two secretaries, one receptionist and...well you get my drift. The attorney in this environment usually attempts to keep personal contact with his or her client to a bare minimum. You end up communicating mostly with their assistants and secretaries by phone, email or text.

The "Just To Get A Rep" Attorney

A "Just To Get A Rep" attorney's main objective is to keep their business relationships in tact even at the detriment of their client's reputation. These attorneys are typically more concerned about building their business brand rather than the client's career. Their "brand" is the main focus. Most "JTGR" attorneys operate with a "go with the flow" attitude in hopes of things developing into the something positive. Selfishly, their goal is to gain success based on the blood, sweat and tears of their clients in hopes of creating a positive perception within the industry. Let's say as a beat maker, you land an opportunity to produce a song for a highly successful recording artist. A highly respected law firm with an extensive client roster also represents the recording artist. In an attempt to get the best possible deal for it's client, the attorney for the artist offers your attorney a deal that is considerably lower than your market value. Your attorney doesn't want to "ruffle any feathers" or show any resistance towards the deal. He or she fears that could ruin the positive working relationship between attorneys or even cause the firm to retaliate in future deals. In order to keep everyone satisfied *except you*. Your "JTGR" attorney does everything in his or her power to convince you to take the deal.

The "Big Thinker" Attorney

A "Big Thinker" attorney seeks out to do right based on their own personal values, while still being sensitive to the values of others. Decisions are made based on truth, rationalization, and objectivity rather than his or her personal gain. They are not motivated by fame or the success generated by their clients. Climbing the ladder to success especially in unethical ways is not the way the "Big Thinker" attorney conducts business. As a prospective client, you need an attorney who can think big and see your vision. With a "Big Thinker" attorney, you can be creative both musically and legally. Let's say you are offered a huge opportunity to produce music for a mega-star. The mega star and its law firm have a history of offering bad deals to producers. Not surprisingly, they also offer what you and your attorney agree is a terrible deal. Unlike the "JTGR" attorney, the "Big Thinker" will do two things: He or she will suggest that you decline the deal or he or she will draft a deal that is applicable to all parties involved. There is no middle ground or room for an unfair type of deal.

The "Homeboy" Attorney

A "Homeboy" attorney doesn't fit the stereotype of a typical attorney. He or she loves the fame of being in the game. He or she wants to interact with its clients as often as possible. The professional and personal lines are often blurred which has an affect on his or her job performance. "Homeboy" attorneys will attempt to develop a personal friendship with their clients while still performing its legal duties. "Homeboy" attorneys enjoy perks and benefits of having you as their client but will also find a way to charge you for everything that happens *out of the office* too. For example, let's say you and your attorney go out one evening for dinner. You happen to ask him or her a question of a legal nature. Although you asked the question in an informal setting, you could receive a bill charging you for receiving legal advice. Don't allow the lines to be crossed or blurred in this way. Keep the two relationships, business and pleasure separate. It will be less complicated and help keep your professional relationship free from unnecessary tension.

The Power Broker Attorney

"Power Broker" attorneys possess mastery skills in negotiation. They have the shrewd negotiation skills needed to construct the perfect deal. "PB" attorneys are critical thinkers that have the drive to make things work while coming up with alternative solutions without defying logic. Taking the high road during negotiations is not an option mainly because it's more important for "PB" attorneys to prove to everyone what is morally right. This can become time consuming for clients in need of fast turnaround times. For example, you and your attorney are satisfied with 95% of a deal being offered. In your view, the 5% at issue is a minor point in which you are willing to concede. A "PB" attorney will fight aggressively to overturn the remaining 5% to be in your favor, even if instructed not to.

It's imperative that you develop a procedure and an acceptable form of communication between you and your attorney specifically when it pertains to strategic planning. You should work closely with your attorney to develop a strategy for each deal, small or large. You should also be updated during each phase of the negotiation period to assess the progress. Most attorneys communicate their strategic points by using what is referred to as "Mark-ups."[2] It allows attorneys to share their thoughts, give suggestions and offer advice at each deal point. Correspondence between you and your attorney can be done through email, video chat, physical mail and personal consultation.

So, Now What?

As a prospective client, you should use these categories as a reference to find the right attorney for you. Not all attorneys fit into just one category. A "Hollywood" attorney may display a "larger than life" persona but still be a "big thinker." The "Homeboy" attorney's "down to earth" personality may create a more productive atmosphere during the negotiation process. Finding an attorney who possesses a combination of styles and skills acceptable to you may be challenging but absolutely necessary. Before doing a search for an attorney, be realistic and clear on what your needs are. Your expectations should be reasonable and in accordance with your current career status. As an aspiring beat maker, it may be impracticable for you to garner the attention of a "Hollywood" attorney without having a respectable track record.

---

2 The term "Mark-ups" refers to the act of reviewing and editing documents.

Fees & Compensation

Entertainment attorneys can earn their salaries based on a number of factors. For the most part, an attorney's track record, reputation and experience will determine the value of salary and compensation an attorney can demand. A strong personality and unconventional style may also add value to an attorney's pay scale. That being said, an attorney's salary is also dependent on the individual's payment preference of his or her firm. The most common payment options you will need to evaluate when hiring your attorney are: hourly rate, contingency, and retainer.

Hourly Rate

Paying a attorney at an hourly rate is pretty straightforward. An attorney is paid for services on an hourly basis. It is important to understand that attorneys will charge you an hourly rate based on ALL services done under your agreement. Services may include drafting and reviewing agreements, phone and email communication, faxing, meeting & conferencing, etc. An attorney may charge you a pro-rated fee for a 5-minute phone conversation on the phone. An attorney will also charge you the postage stamp fee for a letter he or she mails YOU. I only recommend this type of arrangement for deals that require less than ten hours of legal work.

Contingency

A contingency is a fee, which requires a portion of the contract, or settlement goes to your attorney. This type of payment arrangement is actually the industry standard. At first glance, this may seem like a lopsided arrangement but in certain deal situations it can be very beneficial. Larger deals take more time to structure and negotiate which over time can become very costly. A contingency fee allows an attorney to receive compensation as a percentage of the over all deal (which usually contains a financial advance payment). Let's assume you are presented with a production contract worth over $100,000 in future payments. If you arrange for your attorney to receive a 5% contingency fee, he or she will receive the $5000 payment once the deal is consummated. This payment arrangement may save you money in the long run compared to paying an hourly rate.

Retainer

A retainer fee is a fixed amount of money paid by the client in advance to secure the services of an attorney. If you anticipate having a large legal load for your attorney, this may be your best option. Imagine you are working on four different projects over a four-month period. Each project requires legal assistance. In anticipation of the upcoming workload, your attorney requires you to pay an advance fee to assure that services will be paid for. In some cases, the retainer fee may also save a client some money. For example, an attorney may agree to accept a $3000 retainer fee per month. A client may only require legal work on a deal worth $100,000. The deal may also require 10-12 hours of legal work at $250 per hour. With the contingency arrangement, the attorney would be owed a $5000 contingency payment (5% contingency fee of $100,000). By using the retainer fee arrangement, the client was able to save up to $2000 by being changed an hourly rate.

The Attorney For You

There are three skills that your attorney needs in order to be effective and work towards success. He or she needs to be a highly skilled communicator, negotiator and educator. With these skills, your attorney's personality and style is less important in terms of getting the job done for you. After all, getting the job done is what really matters.

Communication is absolutely necessary. Having integrity and the ability to deliver bad news is important. If the deal isn't in their client's best interest, they're not afraid to tell their clients not to force the issue. Don Cannon offers his view about communication:

> I was never the bigheaded artist screaming *I need to speak to Theo right now*! I don't need all that. I just need to speak to my point person and Theo will call me back to let me know everything is good and I can move on with my business. So, it's about putting people in the right spots."[xviii]

A positive attorney/client relationship is essential to maximize turnaround time, minimize delays and maintain value in your career.

Negotiation skills are crucial. Most successful deals are accomplished by the work and preparation done beforehand. When you are well prepared, you are much more confident to negotiate the best deal. Your attorney should share the same goals and be willing to collaborate with you to develop winning strategies. During negotiations, a crafty attorney may be able to structure deals that provide certain tax advantages by deferring payments of royalties, advances or fees. If you feel like a deal is unfair and your have reached your "bottom line," your attorney must be ready to walk away. Knowing current industry trends can help negotiate favorable contracts too.

Education is essential and key to an attorney attracting prospects and keeping current clients. Your attorney should be your independent teacher of all music, business and entertainment related matters. As a prospective client, you should be well informed about your attorney's educational background and any other relevant information that may help during your evaluation. If an attorney is apprehensive about displaying this information on their website or during discussions, he or she may not be the attorney for you anyway.

Attorneys are special individuals with distinct personalities, skills and education. Their "know-how" allows them to take on work that is technically and ethically demanding. Attorneys also have different personalities and use various styles to approach their work. No matter whom you choose, your lawyer must be able to educate and maintain open lines of communication with you. Communication via email or phone should be acceptable. They should be able to educate you in detail about all related subjects. Do your research by speaking with colleagues, music executives or any individuals who may have some insight that can help. Most importantly, speak with other producers who may share the same experiences and concerns. Being a member of a producer community can provide additional resources for not only finding a great attorney but for all music and business matters.

Accountants & Business Managers
(The Numbers Man)

"Everybody wants a new car that makes a status statement. The question is do you buy a Mercedes or a more affordable Honda?"

If you're anything like me, you have probably had the same big dreams about winning the lottery for millions of dollars. Once those thoughts come to mind, you start getting excited about the material things you can buy and how your lifestyle will change. We have all sat around and had conversations about the lottery that usually starts with someone saying *if I had a millions dollars right now I would*...But let's be honest, most of us wouldn't know how or where to even cash a check of such a large amount. Do you deposit a $300 million check into your personal savings account? What about Uncle Sam? Do you know how to properly file your taxes with the IRS having such a large gross amount? These are questions that can be answered by accountants and business managers. However, finding the *right* accountant or business manager is the hard part. Saving you money, helping you make the right investments and planning for the future are important factors of maintaining your wealth as well as leaving an inheritance behind. Selecting the right people to help you with these decisions should not be taken lightly.

Accountants

The most important thing that you need handled when making substantial amounts of money in this industry is an accountant. When you're "hot," the checks can come quickly and they can be extremely large. It's your responsibility to pay taxes out of those checks regardless of when and how they come. An accountant can ensure that you pay that money immediately and that you get all the exemptions due to you. Accountants can keep the producer from incurring tax liabilities in different states or countries. All accountants aren't created equal though. You should definitely choose a certified accountant who has a positive track record and who is familiar with the inner-workings of the music industry. Once you find an accountant you are comfortable working with, make sure you keep your financial records organized to allow him or her to do the best possible for you.

Business Managers

Business management is a profession specifically designed to help clients manage finances. Business managers are involved in all the important aspects of a beat maker or producers business and personal life. Sometimes business managers are also accountants.

Though you will need an accountant to pay your taxes, you only need a business manager if you make an excessive amount of money and your business is active and the earnings are steadily increasing. The business manager/accountant usually gets about 5 percent of the artists gross income. The smart choice is to take responsibility and handle your own finances until you can no longer manage. This is the wisest choice because no matter how much you trust or depend on your business manager, he or she will have other clients and therefore utilize other staff for your routine needs. Your personal life and everything you do in it revolves around your finances at some point, therefore the manager is involved in your personal affairs as they relate to money. Services they may provide are: bookkeeping, tax planning, identifying financial goals and defining realistic business opportunities. They can collect checks, secure mortgages, obtain insurance, make bank deposits, and pay bills while protecting and growing your profits.

If the business manager is recommended to you, make sure that you fully investigate and approve the person based upon your own judgments and needs. A relationship with a business manager is way too intimate and important to rely solely on someone else's opinion. Make sure that the business manager you select has an adequate amount of experience, a solid reputation and a proven track record that you can trust. The income that you have acquired should be used efficiently and invested wisely under the direction of the business manager after your approval. They should have experience in public relations, economics, tax, accounting, auditing, finance and law. A proven track record within the music industry is good but not necessary. Some managers build a reputation off of one successful client and later after building an impressive clientele list, people find out they have been undeserved and or neglected. Make wise and informed decisions in the beginning and you won't regret it at the end.

Do You Need a Business Manager?

When your song becomes a hit, your financial circumstances may change dramatically. Money will be coming in faster than you can spend it. You may be able to buy things you *only dreamed of before*. But, having money and resources can suddenly also lead to impulsive spending. Most newcomers to the industry may want to buy things that are, shall I say *industry standard:* material items like high-end jewelry, automobiles, houses, expensive studio equipment, computers and more. To some, buying these items serve as confirmation that they have finally reached a high financial status.

Buying and showcasing these items also makes a statement. A new car makes a statement that you've "made it" to observers. The question is, should you buy a Mercedes or a more affordable Honda? One of the biggest buys at the top of the list is usually a home. Whether you're buying, leasing or renting finding a new place to live is expensive. When one is buying a house you have to have a down payment. If you're renting the house and you have bad credit, you may have to pay at least three months of rent up front. Let's not overlook the cost of paying a realtor and furnishings. These are decisions that need to be handled responsibly to guarantee your financial future is prosperous.

This is where your business manager comes in. Keep in mind that *business managers are not a necessity.* If you do decide to hire one, remember: *a business manager works for you.* You are the boss and all final decisions should be yours. Remain informed and don't be intimidated to ask questions when it comes to your financial transactions. Always conduct your own research while making decisions and investments. You might not understand every aspect, but having some prior knowledge and being able to refer to facts will assist your decision making process.

The "Hollywood" Business Manager

"HB" managers have a long roster of celebrity clients. They are familiar with Hip-Hop culture and stay up-to-date with current industry trends. *Translation*: They understand their clients spending habits. It's not uncommon for their clients to spend large amounts of money on expensive cars, jewelry and other frivolous material items to present the perception of being wealthy. After all, this is entertainment right? The land of the glitz and glamour, correct? "HB" managers may have resources that make it a little easier for clients to make major buys. For example, they may have a network of automobile dealerships and jewelry merchants preselected for their clients to spend money with. If you want to buy a new Mercedes Benz, the manager will make a "power call" to his or her car dealer friend to work out the arrangement for you. The perception is that the "HB" manager will facilitate a quick and painless transaction for you. Although you may benefit with a quick transaction, the financial benefit may not be yours in the long run. By referring clients to vendors, the "HB" manager is able to maintain a positive working relationship to benefit him or herself and future clients.

The "Efficient" Business Manager

"EB" managers perform every aspect of their jobs at high levels. "EB" managers are experts in tax planning, business planning and networking. They will prepare tax returns and offer important advice particularly during the planning stage of a new business. Once the business is operational, "EB" managers usually take on the role of a general business consultant and trusted advisor. Having a person who can tell you what makes financial sense or not is a real asset. "EB" managers are also great sources for referrals and networking. They may be able to refer professionals such as attorneys, bankers, insurance brokers and even recording artist and label executives. The most important function "EB" managers perform for their clients is being a problem solver with issues concerning cash flow and revenue streaming.

My Story

When I graduated from college on May 21 in 1997, I had no idea what my career would be. I knew what I wanted to do but *how and when would it happen*? I didn't have many options: Plan A was to get a position at a record company. Plan B was to get any type of employment that was paying. To top it off, I had no real plan on how I would make it happen, but I knew I needed to work in the music business. From the blessings of God, I was offered a production and publishing deal about four months after graduation. The two deals were worth more than $100,000 collectively. I was in a really great position financially. I could afford to buy the things that I wanted. However, I really didn't know the best moves to make with that amount of money. I didn't think I was rich but I did think I was financially set to build a foundation of wealth.

The first week I received my check, I was so excited that I contemplated buying a used Range Rover for $44,000 in cash. Cam' Ron had recently bought a Mercedes Benz right after receiving his advance from signing a recording contract with Untertainment Records. Under the peer pressure and my own desire to show off, Cam' Ron and I drove out to a car dealer in Queens, NY in search of a good deal on a vehicle. Once we arrived, the car salespersons gave me choices of used high-end vehicles that included a Mercedes Benz, BMW, Range Rover, etc. The closer I got towards signing the paperwork, the more I knew that I was about to make an irresponsible buy. As much as I wanted that black Range Rover with rust-colored leather interior, I passed on making the purchase. I just couldn't believe I was about to spend $44,000 on a vehicle, when just the week before I didn't have 40 bucks to spend on *anything*.

Sensing my inability to handle my finances responsibly, I asked my attorney some questions and he suggested that I hire an accountant and business manager. Under the recommendation provided by my attorney, I sought out a business management firm based out of New York City to help manage my finances. Until that point, I didn't know there was such a thing as a "business manager" who could help me with managing my money. I thought managing money was an accountant's job. With a positive endorsement from my attorney, I called in and made an appointment to meet with the firm.

    I remember the day I walked into the tall skyscraper located in midtown Manhattan. The business firm located on the eighth floor was divided into departments. There were members specializing in estate planning, investments and tax preparation. The firm seemed to have a great reputation based on an impressive client roster. The firm's clientele consisted of many popular and successful urban recording artists and celebrities. I remember saying to myself, *these guys must be doing something right if all of these big time clients trust them with their money.* If the firm was good enough to handle that caliber of professionals then they must be good enough for me to trust, *right?*

    I soon found out the hard way that my assumptions were far from the truth. I felt very uncomfortable after meeting a few of the team members, when I was whisked away into an office to meet my *assigned advisor.* He, along with his assistant instantly pushed all sorts of documents in my face to sign. They also needed important personal documents from me such as my social security card, driver's license and birth certificate. He went on to explain the services provided to me and what expectation they would also have of me. At that time, the expectations were for me to have a good amount of savings in the bank. I assumed that I would be able to live off of those funds for a while.

    After setting up personal and business banking accounts with the firm's "chosen bank," we had a discussion about my potential recurring monthly expenses. I was in debt like most college graduates. I owed the university money as well as federal government student loans. I had overdue credit card bills and thanks to my ex-roommates, I was also responsible for back rent and utility bill payments. Signing a deal couldn't have come at a better time for me. In my heart, I knew I needed the structure and guidance a business manager would provide but I still had a difficult time dealing with not being able to spend my money the way I saw fit. I wanted to buy things but I didn't want debts collectors to prevent me from doing so. I knew my new business management team would help me resolve those matters, so I thought.

    After a few days, I got up the courage to schedule a meeting with my business manager. In the meeting, I expressed my desire to make a few purchases that seemed to be ordinary at that point in my career. I wanted a new place to live and a new car! Just like I predicted, the business manager wouldn't recommend that I make the purchases "then." Since it was my money and my decision to make, he couldn't prevent me from spending my own money. Even though he tried to persuade me not to go through with it, he still provided me with the resources to get the best deals on my purchases.

Now, was it a smart decision to run out and get a car and a three-bedroom rental house? Of course not! Did it feel good? Absolutely! Not only was I able to move but I was able to help members of my family move as well. My grandmother who lived in New York City housing was able to take pleasure in suburban living, which she enjoyed tremendously. Helping my family made me feel accomplished. Although my business manager tried to dissuade me from making the purchases, he never fully explained why they were bad decisions at the time. Do you know why? There are a few reasons but the most important was all about the money. In my case, the business management firm had already made 5% ($5,000) commission of the $100,000 I earned. Now are you thinking, *$5,000.00 of 100,000 - that's not a lot!* Think about it in terms of what they had to do, or *didn't* have to do. They did very little with my first earnings except take their cut. There were no investments made, no future financial planning, nothing done to help maintain my earnings that justified cutting a $5,000.00 check. The lesson here is: don't just follow the norm, do what will keep the most money in your pockets and whatever works for you.

Business Management Firm Commission

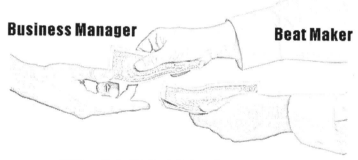

Business Manager

Beat Maker

5% of $100,000=$5,000!
(Business Manager Commission)

What is different about the amount of services and the personal attention that you receive compared to A-list Clientele?

Example #1

Pharrell wants to buy a new car that cost $90,000. He calls up his business management firm to make them aware. A typical response from them would be *what kind of car and how much does it cost*. After realizing that he's about to blow a lot of money they attempt to slow him down in an effort to find him a better purchase price as well as the best interest rate possible. They use their contacts at the bank and other car dealers to find him a better deal.

Example #2

You're an up and coming producer whose starting to make good money but not at millionaire status yet. You call your business management firm and tell them about a $20,000 car purchase you want to make. They ask you how much, are you sure you don't want a lease and what is the car dealers number.

Well, what's the difference?

They are finding better rates and investing time in Pharrell's deal. In your case they may try to do some quick negotiations with the car lot you are at, but no time will be invested into saving you cash outside of your monthly note. To the firm, saving Pharrell $10,000 on a purchase is a bigger deal because they can prove their worth and the value of services to him. Even though you both are making the same purchase, there are vastly different costs involved. Saving $10,000 for Pharrell is quite commendable whereas saving $1,500 for the up and coming producer doesn't warrant the same kind of excitement or praise. For you and your wallet, it does warrant considerable attention; for them and their firm, not so much. The firm's goal is to always preserve the high-end clientele sometimes to the detriment of the up and coming clients. You would think that as an accountant/business management firm, the challenge would be increasing the earnings and satisfaction of the lower end clients. After all, the ones with the millions are already rich and just need to maintain that status. You will quickly find that your new income and tax bracket is special and important to only YOU.

Make the Best Decision for You

During my time at this firm, I learned that the people - attorneys, managers, accountants and the like, all put their best talents and efforts including time and interests towards the A-list clientele. Meaning, if you're not a client at that firm making millions of dollars, you will get way less attention than the higher earners. To some professionals reading this book, the norm is that A-list clientele typically receive more attention than new talent. To a newcomer, paying the same percentage and not receiving the same services like an A-list client may sound absurd and unfair. Despite your newfound wealth, remember that paying the same percentage doesn't guarantee you the same treatment as an A-list client.

Making less doesn't necessarily mean that you pay less. Most business managers charge a percentage and that percentage doesn't always change based on how successful you are. Of course everything can be negotiated but in deals such as these, with established and reputable firms, there is a *standard*.

Choose a business manager or financial advisor who understands tax law and is very knowledgeable about industry trends. As the leader of your team, it will be imperative to make sure your business manager and attorney work together to assure that your financial plan is successfully implemented. Most entertainers, actors, celebrities, performers and musicians develop very close relationships with their business managers. Remember, your accountant or business manager will be the person who you'll have to trust to handle very important financial matters. It's also very important to find a business manager who is an expert in real estate matters, business setup, automobile purchasing as well as touring and appearances. Their knowledge of the inner-workings of the Hip-Hop industry is what makes business managers for entertainers so unique. Experienced business managers know what special issues beat makers and producers will be faced with and should work hard to minimize any financial damage for its clients.

No matter who you hire, always remember that you are in charge of your own finances. As part of your overall long-term plan, the formula for financial success is built around three stages: accumulation, transition and retirement. During the accumulation stage, you will be making beats, which will bring in revenue. Hopefully, your income from making beats will be substantial enough to earn a living. At this point, you shouldn't live beyond your means by buying things you really can't afford, this is the transition stage. The transition stage can last for a few days to a few years depending on your level of success. Your long-term goal should be to live a long happy life after your production career has ended. (See the illustration below.)

BEAT MAKER'S CAREER PLAN

Family & Friends

(Pickup Game Players)

Your family and friends play a very important role in life, both personally and professionally. These are usually the people who are there for you in your time of need providing unconditional support in various ways. As I mentioned earlier in the book, my mom supported my ambitions by providing the music equipment I needed to work on my craft. My uncle and grandfather were my mentors and provided me with a wealth of knowledge and wisdom. During high school, my friends always encouraged me to work on my music skills and become a professional. Even today, my close friends continue to be the people that I count on for their objective opinions and open honesty.

Family and friends can fill a void and provide much needed support to a beat maker or producer embarking on a life-altering career in music production. Having a support system to keep you grounded and focused on your goals is essential. In some cases, you may find the need to alter or even discontinue your relationship with certain family and friends because of their opinions and perceptions of your music profession. To some family and friends, your dream job is a lucrative and glamorous position that they may potentially benefit from. The phrase "don't forget where you came from" will take on a whole new meaning when it appears that you've made it big in the music industry. Your success equals their success. This reasoning may cause family and friends to "flip the script" on you, become demanding, and make unrealistic requests for personal wants and needs.

Let's face it, nowadays when you say you're a beat maker, people aren't that impressed by the title. Anyone can go out and buy some music equipment and then call him or herself a beat maker. The title in itself isn't a prestigious one to hold without some sort of track record. If you actually land a major opportunity and do production-work on a record that's in heavy rotation on the radio, the tables can quickly change. Your name will finally be attached to a professional music project. People are now able to associate you with a popular hit song that they know. Your family may brag: *You heard that new song by Jay Z? My nephew created that song for him.* Your friends may boast: *My boy is about to strike it rich!* This is where perception meets reality.

No matter what career you choose, you may always have a need to help out your family and friends. The difference in the entertainment industry, specifically music, is you're *expected* to do just that. Providing support and financial relief are built in expectations and the demands are high. People close to you don't just want bus fare; they want enough money to buy a new car. Can you think of any other profession where the expectations of the employee to provide or splurge are so high? These high expectations can be stressful on the producer.

In most jobs, an employee receives a check every week or every other week. In the music industry the checks don't come as frequently, nor are they on a schedule. When the checks do come, they are usually larger than a weekly or biweekly check so it gives people a sense that you earn and have more than they do. Even if you don't reveal the dollar amount of your incoming checks, the perception of being in the music industry may cloud their judgment. Music checks aren't usually guaranteed unless it's a royalty check and even then, those checks are mostly based on sales or airplay. Explaining this to family and friends could be a difficult task. Despite knowing how you get paid, when they hear your records on the radio or find out you're working with a high profile artist; you become rich in their minds. The fact that your check has to last you for long periods of time may be difficult to explain to your friends, and a hard concept for them to grasp. Still friends and family are important to your life, as they are able to keep you grounded professionally. You will need to learn how to balance your personal and financial affairs while making clear to your family and friends your intentions.

Family & Friends with Benefits

Beat makers and producers can benefit from having good friends around. Friends and family get to reap many benefits that they might have never experienced without the producers talent. Producers have the opportunity to travel and attend exclusive events; in that respect, friends or family may be exposed to those high profile events and accommodations based on their affiliation with a beat maker or producer. A producer can create many opportunities to benefit friends and family including jobs and careers. Producing is a business and with every successful business, job positions become available. Producers can employ the people around them to do tasks that they may no longer be able to do especially if the business is growing.

In no shape or form am I advising you to employ everyone around you. I am saying that those friends in your circle that you trust and are around all the time can become vital to your success. Use their skills to best suit your business needs. It started with friendships, but if more is going to develop, you must groom them to become successful business relationships. They won't freeload off of you and you won't abuse their friendship if you help develop a healthy business relationship. You want your friends and family to understand what your business needs of them are and what their specific tasks will be. They must understand the importance of their function so that they won't take the position or job for granted. If the goal is success, and you pair your friends or family members with the right employment opportunity, then all should go well.

Don't make your friend who doesn't get out of bed until four every afternoon your personal assistant. You will never get anything accomplished. The failure to recognize one's inabilities and shortcomings will rest on your shoulders. Resist the pressure to give certain jobs to people because they feel like they're close to you or deserve the job. If your big sister, "T" has always thought of you as her little brother who gets on her nerves and she doesn't have to listen to your opinion or do what you say, decides that she wants to be your manager, you probably should think twice about hiring her. Will "T" take orders from you? Do you really want her calling out your childhood nickname at work, in meetings or while passing you the phone? Will you be able to keep her friends out of your office space? Will she be able to handle herself with professionalism and show you respect? Will she keep your business private or will she tell everybody else in the family?

Questioning the dynamics of a relationship when hiring a family member or friend is very important. As an employer, you have to maintain a level of respect in the music industry. Award jobs to those who can successfully accomplish your needs. Also remember to separate business from pleasure. Keep more of a business demeanor during business hours, and then personal feelings and attitudes (possibly issues not related to work) won't easily work their way into the office or business meetings.

On The Job Training

As previously mentioned, professional producers can potentially provide opportunities for employment to close friends and/or family members. In most situations, these jobs can develop into very long and productive career. If you select your friend to manage your business affairs, he or she may be learning on the job, but performing to such a high degree of excellence that other people in the industry take notice and want to hire him or her too. "On the job training" could lead to employees achieving their own business opportunity in the industry. The opportunity was presented through a friendship but hard work and effort led to it becoming a career. This is the ideal way that you want all of your relationships with family and friends to develop. They start out managing you but end up with a clientele list that enables them to provide for themselves as well as employ others. That's a win for everybody.

Beware of Associations

Just as we speak of friends being given jobs or career opportunities and succeeding at them, there are some individuals who are tossed into jobs without clear direction. I advised you to find jobs or specify task for your friends and family that suit their skill set. You never want to give someone responsibilities he or she can't handle. Things can go wrong because of various reasons. Sometimes it's because they are trying to please everybody and other times it's because they don't know how to run a business. In most cases when you hire someone not prepared or willing to learn the job, they have to be fired at some point or the producer may have big fallout with the person. Some very successful producers have the ability to pay people who are close to them but aren't really skilled or able to complete the job.

Let's say super producer "Jay Boog" gave his first cousin, "Shawn" the title of personal manager. Shawn doesn't have any skills, he's inadequate at the job, uninterested and the other staff members have to clean up his errors constantly. The producer really has another personal manager, "Tonya", who carries out these functions to make his life and business go smoothly. People behind the scenes understand it's really the personal manager Tonya who's in the background getting the job done. To everybody on the outside, the family member who falsely portrays himself as the personal manager gets credit for a job well done.

This can be a horrible situation for the up and coming producer who's looking for a personal manager. Just as producers create opportunities that can turn into careers for their family and friends, other people are looking to get rid of dead weight. Producer "Jay Boog" had been paying two people for one job. He's urging Shawn to find something new; Shawn wants him off his back. Shawn starts looking for clients using his cousin's fame and success to bolster his capabilities. In Shawn's mind he's learned so much (he just doesn't do it), he knows what it takes, he can make it on his own and he wants to do it bigger and better.

Here comes the newbie who needs representation. You can't go wrong looking for help from camps that are established right? If you don't make people prove themselves to you it can lead to major downfalls, like hiring Shawn. If you sign a management contract with Shawn specifying calendar years and payment in terms of a percentage of your income, you're in big trouble. Shawn sees that you have promise and he wants to befriend you. He wastes no time bragging to you about how much he does for his cousin the super producer. He can't wait to tell you about all his connections and how he can get you linked in with everything "Jay Boog" is doing. Not only can Shawn get you linked in but he can also he can introduce you to all the heavyweights in the game. You are getting excited because Shawn is telling you everything you want to hear and you can't believe that somebody of his caliber wants to manage and work with little old you! A super producers manager wants to help guide your career. Continue with caution and be aware of other people's garbage!

This person appeared to be successful but that was only based on his affiliation. "Jay Boog" actually had someone else who really watched over Shawn and completed his job. To everybody on the outside looking in, it appears that Shawn was great at his job when in actuality others are picking up the pieces and making it work.

Some people who enter the music industry are attracted to the allure of fame. They also assume that associating with the same group of industry people will make them appear to be "official" or "valid." Without doing the proper research, you may end up with the first cousin, high school friend or associate of an artist who has no work ethic, no skills, but a new title: *your manager*. Be careful!

Balancing Music and Personal Life

Balancing your personal life with your professional career is a complex issue that beat makers and producers often overlook. In most cases, your family is the support system that will be there during all your struggles, both personally and professionally. Having a supportive family is great, but it may also comes with some extreme challenges, some of which we have previously discussed.

What are your main goals and objectives for your professional career and personal life? Do you have a spouse, a significant other, children or relatives that need your specific attention? These are some questions you have to clearly answer so that you can begin to create a balance for all parties involved. When you think about how you spend a typical day, how do you divide your time? Most people spend the majority of their day at work or school with an additional hour or two for travel and preparation time. As a beat maker you will need more time to be creative and perform your job to a high degree. Our jobs aren't structured the way a typical nine to five would be. However, there are some similarities. You should treat music production as a job. Approach it having dedicated hours that you will work and complete music tasks within a certain time frame.

Digging for samples, organizing sounds, developing programming skills are a few elements of beat making that take a considerable amount of time. It is important to specify an allotted time for these elements and with beat making in general to create a working platform. Dedicated time is one of the hardest things to do if your family doesn't view it as a job, even if they understand it can potentially pay the bills. They see you working from a home studio and feel like you can start and stop whenever you choose. You have to keep the balance and draw a line. You don't want somebody stopping you in the middle of your creative process to go and buy some dish washing liquid. You may not get that creative zone back so easily; in fact, you may lose the whole creative vibe. You don't want to come back from the store, lose the creative vibe that you were in and be upset at whoever sent you to run that errand. Yo may avoid this by communicating *clear defined boundaries*. If you take your job seriously, your family will have no other choice but to treat it with the same respect.

If you want to have enough time for work and family without expending great effort, you need to create a strategic plan. As an independent beat maker or producer you are working for yourself. The boundaries and planned schedule gives the producer a working structure that his or her family and friends will adapt to. These boundaries and schedules will soon become unspoken rules.

Most producers starting out have nine to five jobs, part time employment or are enrolled in school. It will become a challenge to balance current employment, family life and your music career. With that in mind, you will have to make sacrifices for your music. The creative process deserves specific effort and dedication, and if you love it as I do, you won't feel right until you are in the lab (studio). The creative time should be just as important as the nine to five. If you have plans on replacing a full time job with a career in music production, you must be prepared to make great sacrifices. The hardest part is determining what should be forfeited. You will have to work twice as hard, party less, see your girlfriend or boyfriend on a limited basis, which can sometimes create other issues. Your significant other may start to question the relationship. "Is music more important to you than I am? When are you going to start putting me first?" Don't be shocked when these questions are hurled at you. Be prepared to answer them. The truth is, you are investing in your career rather than focusing on maintaining a job. Consider if getting in a relationship while your trying to enter this game is possible or even an option. With investments come sacrifices that hopefully, will pay off in the end. Hopefully, if you have a significant other, they will provide you with the necessary support while your building your career. Once your career is defined, you'll have other things to consider when it comes to family. You'll have to protect their privacy and make sure people don't use them to get to you.

A&R's (General Managers)

*I hate a bandwagon ass A&R or a "yes" man. The ones who are
always looking for the same type record that another big name
producer has out! -Nottz*

Once you have assembled a Dream Team, it's time to finally
play the game against some industry players and teams. The first team
you will encounter within the music industry is the A&R department.
The A&R (Artist and Repertoire) department is the division of the record
label or publishing company responsible for finding and nurturing new
talent. The A&R division and its members are also responsible for
finding collaborators like you, the beat maker or producer. As a beat
maker or producer, it's imperative that you build a positive working
relationship with A&R representatives or members of the department. If
you plan to pitch your music to major label artists, the A&R people are
who you need to contact. Now, here comes the fun part. If your strategy
is to collect a list of A&R phone numbers and email addresses from
some sort of directory, try again. Nine times out of ten, they won't accept
your call or respond to your email. Most A&R reps don't accept
unsolicited phone calls, emails or physical mail from people they don't
know. For the most part, this is an industry standard for all record
executives. You would think that an A&R would be eager to connect
with as many young and enthusiastic beat makers as possible. As I will
discuss, A&Rs come in all shapes and sizes with different personalities.
Some A&Rs are passionate about their jobs while others may have
ulterior motives, which influence their actions.

From the outside looking in, the A&R position may seem like a
cool job with unlimited perks. Most A&Rs get to work with superstar
artist and producers, rub elbows with powerful music executives and
attend V.I.P. parties with celebrities. But the A&R position plays an

integral role in music projects. One of the main and toughest responsibilities for an A&R is maintaining positive communication with the artist roster they are assigned to work with. Having the authorization to offer artist and/or producers recording deals is one of the biggest misconceptions about the A&R position. A&Rs scout, recruit and discover artists for the record label, but the signing power is usually delegated to the label head or president of the A&R division. When I say "power," I mean possessing the combination of influence, courage and credibility. An A&R may find the talent, but without the power to influence his or her boss, it will be very difficult to get a recording deal completed. For example, let's assume that an unsigned artist with the commercial potential to become the "next Michael Jackson" walks into an A&R's office; he or she won't be able to sign him without the approval from the president of the A&R division.

A&R Styles & Personalities

The style and personality of individuals who hold A&R positions are important to beat makers and producers looking to build relationships in music. These are the people with the "ears" responsible for finding talent for the record label. In any profession, you will be forced to interact with individuals with unique personalities. A&R representatives are no exception. Here are a few examples of A&R styles and personalities you may come across:

The "Hollywood" A&R

These are young flashy individuals who work at one of the major labels. Without explanation, they aren't accessible to aspiring producers or new talent. It's nearly impossible to obtain direct contact information or make connections through social media. He or she performs their job duties while maintaining a "go-with-the-flow" attitude. The legacy and reputation of the record label is what fuels his or her professional demeanor.

The "Corporate" A&R

These are pro record company establishments. In some ways, they dictate what is presented in the music market place. They view music projects from a business prospective and only seek out talent that will increase their record label's financial bottom line. They understand how the corporate system works and the effect commercial recordings will have on radio programming. Signing artists with minimal talent but commercial potential is his or her main objective.

Quick Story

I had a meeting with a major label corporate A&R (who shall remain nameless). I walked into his plush office and took a seat at his desk. We had a short discussion while I played some tracks in the background. After listening to about 15 tracks, the A&R selected 4 that really got his attention. He seemed very excited and complimented me on my work. I was excited by the track selections he made because I felt like the tracks were creative and would bring a unique sound to any artist on the label's roster.

Without hesitation, he says with excitement, "I just signed a new artist to the record label!"

"Let me check it out," I said.

The A&R continues, "With the proper budget, this young kid is going to sell millions of records."

I asked myself, Budget?

He played about 4 songs by the new artist. As I listened, I remember sitting there asking myself, "why did he sign this kid? This is terrible!"

To be fair, the songs did contain simple but catchy choruses; however they lacked creativity, originality and good lyrical content. The songs sounded like an amateur created them. Around that time, the top

10 songs on the radio had many of the same musical elements in which the new artist was imitating.

At that moment, I realized that the "Corporate" A&R was less interested in my music or any good music for that matter. He was more interested in pushing music that he believed to have commercial appeal and be appropriate for the current radio audience.

The "Homie" A&R

The "Homie" A&R gets it's name from having personal ties to his or her boss. He or she could be a close friend or family member who obtained the position based on recommendations of the boss/supervisor. The relationship between an A&R and boss/supervisor is more like a friendship rather than a professional working relationship. In some cases, the "Homie" A&R may not be an employee of the record company at all. However, he or she may still perform just like an employee because of the friendship with the boss. The "Homie" A&R looks and feels important amongst their peers because of this faux title.

The "Humble" A&R

The "Humble" A&R want to play a very instrumental role in producing good music projects and aren't concerned with receiving any extra accolades. They are not influenced or pressured by a record label's financial circumstances or bottom line. A good product that contains great music is what satisfies the "Humble" A&R.

A&Rs and Good Music

As you can probably imagine, there are unlimited stories and accounts that involve interactions between the A&R and producer. The biggest complaint that I hear from beat makers about A&Rs is their lack of ability to select good music. "I like an A&R who knows good music when he or she hears it and is not afraid to take a chance with good music as well" says producer !llmind. [xix]As a beat maker or producer, your future could depend on the opinion of one individual. An A&R could either provide a beat maker with a huge beat placement opportunity or become a huge roadblock during your journey to success.

Backroom Deals

Before we talk about backroom deals, I want to make this clear: There are many honest and trustworthy people within the music industry that go above and beyond their job responsibilities. With that being said, there are people who are opportunists and take advantage of situations. They may even use their job title and resources for their personal gain. Believe it or not, there are A&R reps (and other label executives) that use their position to "influence," "persuade" or "extort" money in exchange for a relationship with them.

As we know, the A&R department is the division of the label that you, the producer will primarily be in communication with. The fact that the A&R department is the "middleman" between the producer and artist creates a business opportunity for some A&R reps looking to make extra cash. Let's say you get a chance to meet an A&R from Atlantic Records. You play some of your music and they really love it! Next, the A&R would like you to collaborate with Atlantic Records recording artist Trey Songz, *but there is a catch*. You have to agree to give the A&R part of your proceeds.

I know you what you're thinking, *get the hell out of here, they don't do that*. Sorry to inform you that yes, this form of extortion does really happen. Before you reject the idea of giving up a portion of your proceeds, think about if this were your first opportunity at a *major placement*, what would you do then? In the example, the A&R used his position to lure producer into backroom deals to benefit his or herself. This type of arrangement (also referred to as a "kick back") is not a new concept, but over time label employees have developed different ways to set up an "unofficial" structure to continue their self-serving dealings.

Producer Jake One had firsthand experience with "kick backs" in early 2002:

> I had an experience with an A&R guy from DreamWorks. My manager Walt managed to get some beats over to a new artist signed to DreamWorks. He ended up picking some beats so DreamWorks decided to fly me down to Oakland, California to work with him. The A&R proposed a deal that would net me $20,000 per track but only if

the A&R could receive $5,000 per track in return compensation. I had absolutely no problem with it at all since I was only receiving like $200 dollars a track in Seattle, Washington at the time. I knew it was wrong but I thought it was common practice. The A&R was at all the studio sessions and he seemed pretty cool. He had absolutely no clue about Hip Hop at all though. This A&R is still kicking around labels to this day.[xx]

In this situation, it worked out for Jake One because he was still able to gain additional placements elsewhere. His producer's fee also increased dramatically because of the success of the placement. Such success won't always be the case. You won't always be so lucky especially if you build a reputation on making these sorts of transactions. Once you start accepting deals like this, your reputation may prevent you from getting offered a fare or a better deal. A&Rs may start taking advantage of you, which will keep you from getting your "going rate" that you deserved. Why would an A&R pay you $10,000 for a production fee if they know you will accept $5,000 to gain the placement? The lesson here is to maintain a standard that doesn't devalue your production work.

These deals aren't done in some dark, smoke-filled rooms, like some illegal drug deal, but in most cases, in the office or the studio. Of course the transaction is kept secret because it's unscrupulous. A&Rs who conduct backroom deals already receive a salary. Behind their companies back, they are charging inflated fees and keeping a percentage of the producer's money. This deal is also a disadvantage to the artist because the fee comes out of his or her budget, and the artist will eventually have to pay it back. The money being taken by an A&R could be better used to advance the project instead of padding a greedy A&R's pocket.

It wouldn't be in the A&R reps best interest for anyone (especially his or her boss) to know that these types of proposals and arrangements exist. So, instead of meeting at a secret location to collect a brown paper bag full of money, some A&Rs have become more creative. As a legal and ethical alternative, A&Rs launch independent business entities such as a label, production, publishing or management company with the sole purpose of collecting money from sources other than their "day job." This practice amongst A&Rs is not uncommon. While it may seem innocent to most, it's a clear *conflict of interest*. Do you really think an A&R is going to discover the "next Lady Gaga" and deliver her to their major label? I wouldn't bet on it. The same thing rings true for producers too. A&Rs are always looking for a new sound and if you come along with some great music, you may be met with a dilemma. Rather than being placed with a major label, an A&R may try to sign you to their own independent label for personal gain.

The A&R Pathway

A major label A&R can provide a huge opportunity for beat makers and producers to break into the game. Some major labels have artist rosters equivalent to an NFL football team, so there is never a shortage of projects under development. Before you think you can walk in an A&R's office with your music, you may need to meet a certain criteria or "prerequisite" before you're able to play a single note. Remember, A&Rs know they are the middle person between you, the label and most of all, an opportunity. I've heard of several prominent A&Rs refusing to meet with producers who had existing publishing or production deals. I've even heard of an A&R refusing to listen to any music created with a specific music production software program. The worse and most egregious example of unethical behavior by an A&R is hearing about several cases where the A&R asked for production credit to provide the producer with a placement. Yes, it can become a very dirty game, the question is: are you willing to play?

ROYALTIES: How Do I Get Paid?

"As a producer you are paid a royalty based on record sales and copyright ownership."

Let's assume that you and your Dream Team are making some major strides, promoting and pitching your music to industry insiders. Your music is gaining the interest of several major label A&R representatives. A major placement opportunity seems imminent. Your next question should be: *how would I get paid from this opportunity?* Educating prospective beat makers on the way we get paid is one of the main reasons why I decided to write this book. Most aspiring beat makers are not familiar with how the music industry works. It's easy to fall in love with the creative side of production, but if production is your dream job, you need to know how you can benefit financially to make a living. For example, if you apply for an employment position at McDonald's, the job description and responsibilities are straightforward. You will be preparing food, cleaning and providing customer service in exchange for being paid an hourly wage. So, how can you expect to produce music and not know how you will be paid for your services? If you do get paid for your production services, who issues the check? Does the check just appear mysteriously in your mailbox? How was your service fee established? Are you giving away all of your music rights for free? These are questions that should be answered by every beat maker and producer.

The music production profession is demanding and requires a lot of time. Unlike an average wage-paying job, most producers aren't paid an hourly rate. Instead of an hourly rate, producers are paid a royalty through a *royalty system*. A *royalty* is a payment made to a producer or copyright owner in exchange for services or the use of his or her copyright. A *royalty rate* is usually calculated by taking a percentage of the gross or net income based on sales. The royalty rate can also be a *fixed amount* or *penny rate* stipulated in your agreement.

Royalties are paid to the producer and/or copyright owner by a variety of users. Record labels, publishers, distributors, movie production companies, authors and other users all pay royalties in exchange for a license to distribute, manufacture, display and/or reproduce copyrighted work (see "Copyright Ownership" on page 94).

Producers receive payments in a few different ways. They receive upfront advances and various royalty payments. Earnings from record company royalty payments come semiannually. That's right, royalty payments usually *only come twice a year*. Music has to be sold and exploited to generate income for the record labels, publishing companies and copyright owners. As a producer you are paid a royalty percentage based on record sales and copyright ownership. To maximize your potential earnings, you need to maximize the rate of your royalties.

The Four Royalties

Do you think you're going to be rich after selling a million records? Do you think you're going to be making huge royalty check deposits into your bank account? Do you think you get paid each time your music is played on the radio?

These are all questions that usually come to mind when discussing royalties. As you will see, *all royalties are not created equal.* There are four major royalty income streams that all music producers should be very knowledgeable of. If you were car salesmen, you would want to know your salary and commission off of each sale, right? It's very similar in music production. A producer is able to receive a royalty for production work and a separate royalty for being the copyright owner. Let's discuss the four major royalties in detail:

Production Royalty

A production royalty is paid to the producer of a sound recording (the song) by the record label and/or publishing company. For example, a producer will enter into an agreement with a record label or publishing company to "produce" and develop a sound recording or master for an upfront fee and a royalty based on future sales. The producer royalty rate ranges from 2% to 6% of the SRLP (Suggested Retail List Price). As an aspiring or even midlevel producer, you won't be able to negotiate a royalty higher than 3% but don't worry, we will discuss why this will be a mute point later. At first glance, you might think that 3% of SRLP ($17.99) isn't a bad deal; but as you will discover, the royalty rate is actually a formula to help determine your "true" rate or actual money rate. Say you agree to a 3% royalty for production of one master recording, 3% of $17.99 (SRLP) is roughly .54-cents. That's not bad. If you sell 1,000,000 albums, that's over $540,000 for you right? *Not so fast.*

Remember, the royalty rate is a formula to figure out your "actual" rate. That .54-cent per album is the sum of the entire revenue pool, which *all producers will share and split.* So, if there are 12 master recordings on an album, that means the .54-cents will be divided by 12 to determine the rate for each master recording. The .54-cent per album quickly turns into .045-cents when divided by 12. So, after 1,000,000 albums sold, you would receive about $45,000 for each master recording instead of the whopping $540,000. Sorry.

If that's not enough, let's dig a little deeper. I mentioned earlier that a producer could charge an upfront fee for services. These advances can range from $1 to as high as $250,000 for production work on a single master recording. For aspiring and midlevel producers, expect to receive an advance in the neighborhood anywhere between $1 and $10,000 per master recording. Most advance payments are usually recoupable against future royalties, which means you will not receive any royalties *until the advance is repaid.* If you have some bargaining power, you might be able to add a *record one clause* into your agreement, which stipulates: *all royalties will be paid regardless of whether advances have been recouped from the first record sold.*

Continuing with the example above, let's assume that you agreed to produce one master recording for an upfront production fee of $10,000 with a 3% royalty rate. After selling 1 million copies, you would be owed $35,000 in royalty payments. Not bad right?

There is a huge hurdle you will have to climb over before you will be able to get your $35,000 in royalty payments though. Most artist recording deals are structured in a way that prevent any royalties to be paid until all recording cost are recouped - and that includes yours too! We'll discuss artist-recording deals later but understand that you will not get paid any royalties until the entire recording budget is recouped. Some artist recording budgets can exceed well over $1 million dollars. It is perfectly possible for you to sell one million albums and still be owed thousands of dollars royalties. The amount of time it takes to receive royalties is the main reason why there isn't much of a reason to make your royalty rate a major real sticking point during contract negotiations. What's the point of arguing about a fraction of a penny when artist deals are structured in a way that make it nearing impossible to recoup and earn royalties without selling millions of records.

Performance Royalty

A performance royalty is paid to the copyright owner and/or songwriter when a song is performed live or broadcast publicly. Most beat makers and producers are also songwriters and copyright owners. The Copyright Law Of 1976 gives each copyright owner six exclusive rights with one being the exclusive right to perform their composition in public. In simple terms, a performance royalty is a percentage of money paid to a beat maker/copyright owner for the right to play their music in public places such as nightclubs, on the radio, amusement parks, live concerts, etc.

Mechanical Royalty

The record label or music publisher pays a mechanical royalty to the copyright owner. As a copyright owner, you have the right to reproduce and distribute your own work in records; this is known as mechanical rights. The monies paid to copyright owners for the rights to manufacture and distribute your work are called mechanical royalties. So, if you create an original composition, track, beat (or whatever you call it), you are entitled to receive mechanical royalties after granting someone a mechanical license. With the protections allowed under the Copyright Act, once a song has been released to the public, a copyright owner must be paid a specific payment established by the law. Meaning, if someone wants to use your work, they may not need your permission but they will have to pay you. They will have to pay the maximum "statutory rate" provided by the Copyright Act.

Synchronization Royalty

Software, gaming, and television & film production companies pay a synchronization royalty to the copyright owner. A synchronization license gives a music user (or licensor) the right to synchronize (play along) your music in time with images in a motion picture, television show, film, slide show, video game or any visual media. Unlike the three previous royalties, the fees are set based on the importance of the use, the length of the music and the type of media used. There are industry standards that most T.V. and Movie producers follow. For example, usage fees for a song used in a movie may range from $500-$15,000, with popular songs reaching up to as much as $250,000 or even more. Beat makers and producers can earn a substantial income just by issuing synchronization licenses to television & film production companies.

Getting Your Cut!

Your financial future will depend largely on royalty payments generated by various revenue sources. Royalties in theory are deferred payments that are paid and calculated in numerous ways. This is why negotiating royalty share percentages in advance are very important.

As a beat maker or producer, your revenue stream will mainly derive from advance production fees, and royalty payments from music licensing and record sales. No matter what source your royalty income may derive from, do your best to negotiate a sizable royalty share and percentage as part of a long-term financial plan for the future.

Production Deals

Now that you understand the royalty system and how it works, you are now ready to delve into "production deals." To assure that you will receive a royalty, a production deal is required. A *production deal* is an agreement between you, the record label or artist, which explains in detail what services you will provide in exchange for a royalty or fee. The royalty system is what makes most production deals work. Most deals can be straightforward or really complex. It all depends on how the deal is structured.

As a producer, you work countless hours in the studio creating the best music product possible and you also take on other responsibilities especially on the business side. I remember having a late night studio session at the Hit Factory in New York City. In between recording vocals with the artist, I booked future sessions, reviewed production agreements and proposals. Music production consists of everything needed to complete the project such as administrative duties, hiring engineers, hiring background vocalist, clearing samples and much more. Most aspiring artist work with producers who can develop their talents to obtain a major recording contract. In the earlier years, a record company would sign an artist and assign one of its A&R executives to "produce" the records. Today, most record labels hire a producer to oversee the entire production process of an album or single for an artist.

The Artist Recording Deal Triangle

The record label, the artist and the producer are the three main components that construct most production deals. The points of the triangle below are a representation of each component involved in a typical artist-recording contract. The component that lands at the top will be determined by the structure of the deal. (See illustration 3.)

Illustration 3.

Who will be paying you, the recording company, the artist or both? To answer these questions, we must first examine the different types of production deals that are most commonly proposed:

Staff Producer Deal

The record label or company signs an artist and assigns a producer (you) to handle all the production work for the project in-house. It's not uncommon for these deals to be done in country, pop, rock and urban music. Producers receive a salary, a royalty override on sales and production credit on releases. This is a great deal for a producer looking to work as an employee under a typical business structure rather than establishing an independent entity on his or her own.

Production Company Deal

A production company deal is similar to a staff deal but instead of hiring staff producers, the label hires a *production company* to complete the entire project from start to finish. The production company is usually paid an upfront fee and a royalty percentage based on the retail list price of the records sold by the artist. This type of deal is very common, especially in Hip-Hop music. There are major pitfalls for a producer in this type of deal though. If you're the main producer and owner of the production company, this is a sweet deal. If you're a staff producer or beat maker signed to the production company, you may not receive any upfront fees or royalty percentages for your production work.

Standard Production Deal

Independent producers are hired by the record label or artist to produce one master recording or an entire album. Independent producers are usually paid an advance against royalties and a royalty based on the retail price of records sold by an artist. In a typical artist recording deal, the artist is required by the record label to be responsible for hiring and paying the producer fees and royalties. So, even if the record label commissions a producer for a project, the artist will still be legally responsible to pay the producer. Most artist recording deals have a provision that stipulates the royalty percentage an artist will receive on record sales. However, the producer isn't guaranteed a royalty share at all. In order for a producer to receive a royalty share, he or she would need to negotiate with an artist to share in their royalty percentage.

All-In Recording Deal

An "All-In" recording deal gives the artist the responsibility of paying royalties to the producer out of its own royalties. Most artist record deals are structured in this way. As a producer, there are some advantages and disadvantages. One of the advantages for a producer is the ability to negotiate a higher royalty with the artist instead of the record company or label. The record label doesn't want to be responsible for negotiating deals between individuals producer anyway. The artist can offer the producer a better royalty rate because the payment are deducted from his of her royalties. For example, if the artist's royalty is 12% of the suggested retail list price, the producer gets 3%, leaving the artist with a 9% royalty rate. If you have leverage, you may be able to get a larger royalty percentage (usually in the range of 3%-7% royalty rate). In reality, all of these numbers don't mean much if the artist doesn't earn any royalties. That's the MAJOR disadvantage to the producer. In simple terms: *The artist needs to earn royalties in order for you to earn royalties.*

Partnership/Venture Deal

An independent producer or production company may agree to partner with the record label, usually splitting the profits 50/50 after deductions. Most "A-List" producers with a lengthy track record can get a deal with an even profit split. If you're the main producer or the owner of the production company, this could be a very lucrative deal. The record label advances all funds for recording, marketing and promotion budgets for the project in exchange of 50% of the profits.

Fees and Advances

Producers are paid a fee or an advance payment for their production services. The fee can be for additional services such as programming, remixing, pre or post-production. The term *"producer fee"* refers to an advance payment that is recoupable against any future royalties. Although the term may suggest that the fee is a one-time charge, it really is an advanced payment recoupable against future royalties earned. Almost any advance payment made by a record label to the producer will be recoupable against future royalties or any additional payments owed to you.

Recording Funds

The recording fund, also referred to as the *budget*, is a financial budgeting plan set by the record label to produce a music project. This budget is used to allocate funds to an artist for all recording cost and advances associated with the project. For example, a record label may set a $250,000 recording budget for a new artist to complete an album project. If the artist manages to complete the album below the projected budget, the artist can keep the money left over. This is why an artist may attempt to lower the amount of your production fee. The less money an artist has to pay you, the more money the artist can keep in his or her pocket.

Can you guess where this is headed? The producer's advance is truly at the *artist's discretion*. The artist determines how much he or she is willing to pay for your production services. You may have your own standard fee for your services but all artists aren't created equal and neither are all recording budgets. To get the placement, you may need to lower your fee to accommodate an artist's budget.

Prorated Royalties

After reading the previous information about royalties, you might think you have a good understanding of the system, *but not so fast!* All royalty shares pretty much go out the door when royalties are *prorated.* According to the Webster's Dictionary the definition of "prorated" means to "divide, distribute, or assess *proportionately.*" The last word "proportionately" is the word that affects you and your royalty share. As an entry or midlevel producer, your "mechanical" royalty will be reduced depending on how many songs appear on an album. If there are 10 songs on an album's track list and you produced one song, you would get paid one-tenth, which would equal the standard royalty rate. What do you think your royalty rate will be when there are 11 songs on an album? Yes, you would get paid a royalty but it would be reduced or "prorated" as if the album only contained 10 songs. This is because there's a royalty cap or limit on how much a record company is obligated to pay songwriters for their work on a single album. This is referred to as the "royalty cap." The royalty cap or "mechanical royalty pot" is divided or prorated based on the number of songs on an album's track list.

Although mechanical royalties are based on the statuary rate set by the U.S. government, that doesn't mean that the rate can't be reduced. Continuing with the example above, the mechanical royalty pot is determined usually by multiplying the statutory rate by ten songs (9.1 cents X 10 songs).

Why only ten songs? Ten songs also referred to as the "*ten times rate*" is usually added to the *controlled composition clause* to limit the amount of songs delivered by an artist for an album. If an artist were paid 9.1 cents for every song, what would stop him or her from adding 20 songs to double the rate? The answer is absolutely nothing. As you will see, the decision to have 20 songs on a single album will reduce your royalty by 50%.

If your mechanical royalty is based on the 9.1 cents statutory rate, you would receive 2.2 cents (9.1 cents divided by 50% (prorated album rate)=4.5 cents divided by 50% (producer/writer share minus the artist/writer share) =total mechanical royalty of 2.2 cents. So, as you can see your royalty can be reduced from 4.5 cents to 2.2 cents by adding more than ten songs. These numbers can't be changed either. Once you sign the agreement, the percentages are permanent and go on to perpetuity. Even if the statutory rate is increased, you will be stuck with 2.2 cents. (See the illustration 4 below.)

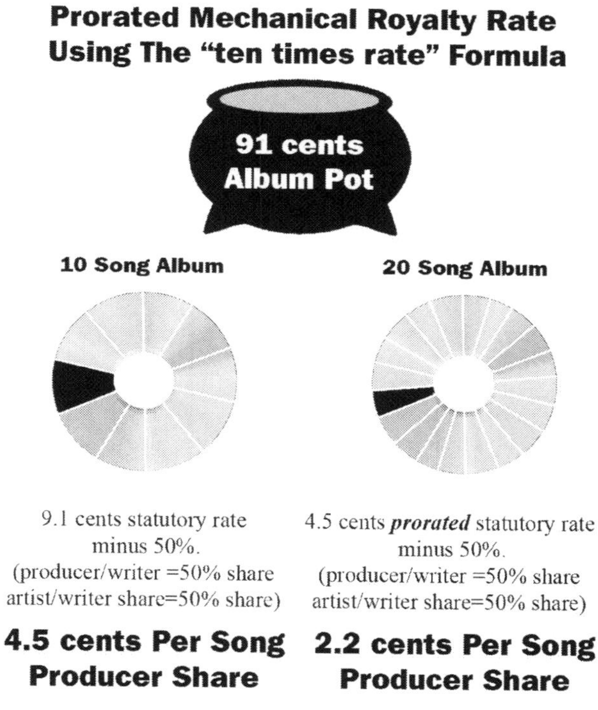

Prorated Mechanical Royalty Rate
Using The "ten times rate" Formula

91 cents Album Pot

10 Song Album   **20 Song Album**

9.1 cents statutory rate   4.5 cents *prorated* statutory rate
minus 50%.   minus 50%.
(producer/writer =50% share   (producer/writer =50% share
artist/writer share=50% share) artist/writer share=50% share)

4.5 cents Per Song   **2.2 cents Per Song**
Producer Share   **Producer Share**

Illustration 4.

If that's not enough for you, can you imagine what would happen to your royalties if you produced a single song on a double album? You guessed it; your royalties will be reduced to a percentage amount that's unimaginable. We'll touch on a real life situation involving the Controlled Composition Clause later. *The Controlled Composition Clause* is a section in your production contract that allows the artist to set a cap limit on the total mechanical share for an album.

As you increase your bargaining power and reach the mid level of your career, you may be able to negotiate a higher mechanical rate. The goal of course is to get the maximum statutory rate without it being prorated or decreased for any reason. Unfortunately, this will be an ongoing battle between you and the record company. Remember, mechanical royalties are monies paid by the record company to a songwriter and are non-recoupable from any advances (in most cases). Record companies can't avoid paying out mechanical royalties but they can certainly attempt to reduce the rate.

Trying to get the record company to agree to a specified amount called a "*penny rate*," is a strategy commonly used to increase your royalty rate. For example, instead of agreeing to a percentage of the statutory rate, try to get the record company to agree to pay you a set rate of 3 cents. Think about it, if your "penny rate" is 3 cents per song and an album sells 1 million copies, you would receive $30,000 in mechanical royalties for each. No need to worry about your royalties being prorated. In addition, you can negotiate to raise the "penny rate" if record sales exceed over 500,000 (certified gold) or 1,000,000 (certified platinum).

Up to this point, we've focused on mechanical royalties, but your "producer" royalties can also be prorated. Unlike mechanical royalties, the U.S. government does not set producer royalty rates! The royalty rate or percentage you receive for your production service is negotiated *between you and the artist*. Because your royalty rate is essentially a percentage of the artist royalty, the artist has room to negotiate and offer you a reasonable rate. If you are just starting out, you will most likely be offered a rate of about 3 percent. This is where things get tricky. As we discussed earlier, your producer royalty rate is a *percentage* of the SRLP but this is also the amount that determines the producer's royalty pot in which ALL producers share. So, if the producer's royalty pot were 80 cents per album you would receive 8 cents per song for an album containing 10 songs. Here is the fun part: *What do you think happens when you have more than 10 songs on an album?* Your royalties are prorated again! Of course, as you become more successful and gain more bargaining power you will be able to receive a higher royalty rate.

Record One Royalties

Unlike artists, producers are customarily paid on all records sold, after the recoupment of any advance payments. These are called *"record one" royalties* because the payments are generated from the first record sold. Most production agreements won't contain this clause for obvious reasons. The record labels aren't happy about paying out any royalties until it has been paid back all recording advances. In theory, the "record one" clause allows producers to receive royalty payments immediately after the recouping all *producer* advances. The artist and their record label will try their best to eliminate this clause from the your deal. Although it may be difficult, with bargaining power you may be able to insert this clause into all of your production deals. After all, some major label recording budgets can exceed $1 million dollars or more thereby making it nearly impossible to repay the advanced royalty payment anyway.

Cross-Collateralization

Just hearing the words *"cross collateralization"* makes me feel a little nauseous. Once you understand the concept, you might start feeling sick as well. In a nutshell, the concept of recoupment is simple: any advance payments made to the producer are recoupable against future royalty payments. So, if a producer receives $5000 as an advanced, he or she won't receive any royalties until the $5000 is recouped. *This is easy arithmetic, correct?*

Let's say you produce two albums: You are paid and advance of $50,000 for Album #1 and $50,00 for Album #2. Let's assume Album #1 earns royalties of $25,000 and Album #2 earns royalties of $75,000. If you do the math and subtract the advances from royalties earned, you will notice that Album #1 is un-recouped by $25,000 and Album #2 is recouped along with a $25,000 surplus (see example below).

In a perfect world, you would receive royalties of $25,000 for Album #2.

If you have a cross collateralization clause built into your deal, you won't receive anything. If the two albums were "cross-collateralized" using the example above, the $25,000 earned from Album #2 would be applied to the account of Album #1 to recoup the $25,000 balance. What do you think about that? Just when you were on the way to earning royalties, a clause is snatching all 25,000 of your dollars away. See illustration 5 below.

Illustration 5.

The Producer Declaration Agreement

A *"Producer Declaration"* is an agreement used by a record label to obtain the ownership rights in master recordings (also referred to as the sound recording) created by the music producer. A record label can't operate unless it has permission from all copyright owners to copy, manufacture and distribute music. So, even if a label hires you to produce a master recording for an artist, the label will still ask you to "declare" or transfer some important rights to "sell records." While standard production agreements may contain the specifics in key areas such as publishing and royalties, the producer declaration focuses exclusively on obtaining master rights.

Think of the master as being the "sound recording" of a musical composition. Before the digital age, musical compositions were recorded on analog tapes. The record company, the owners of the tapes under the "work made for hire" provision (see Beat makers For Hire page 101) were able to reproduce and distribute musical compositions. Today, beat makers and producers use music production software programs that allow users to create musical compositions and create audio files (which are sound recordings). You can create a musical composition without having a sound recording, but you can't create a sound recording without a musical composition. So, each recorded song consists of two separate creative works, both of which are owned or controlled by you.

To get a better understanding, let's say you and a new artist decide to collaborate. The artist is signed to a major record label but you both decide to work together without any label involvement. You guys end up recording several songs at your home studio. One song in particular has the potential to become a hit so the artist let's the record label hear it. The record label loves the song and wants to release the song immediately. What do you think happens next? If you think the record label will just write you a check, you are sadly mistaken. The first thing the label will do is present you with a producer declaration agreement to move forward. This agreement will focus on three areas: master rights, producer fees and warranties.

Master Rights

The record label will need the right to copy or reproduce the master recording created at your home. There are a few ways a record label can obtain this right. The first is by acquiring a license. With a license, the label does not obtain total ownership of the song, but rather certain limited rights to use it. Your options are unlimited. You may decide to give the label the right to manufacture only 10 albums if you like. You may decide to keep all of your music non-exclusive, leaving open the possibility for other labels to make deals with you.

Another way a record label can obtain master rights is by making a "work made for hire." A work made for hire is work prepared by an employee within the scope of his or her employment. So, if a record label hires you to produce a master recording, they in fact are the true owners of the original master recording, not you, the creative one behind the music. We will dive deeper into this later.

Producer Fees

Most declaration agreements will outline the producer's fee and any other additional costs associated with the master recording but pay close attention to this section. Over the years, most major record labels would agree to pay 50% of the producer's fee as a show of good faith to consummate the declaration agreement. Today, major record labels shy away from paying any advance payments at all. If you're not careful, you could be obligated to deliver a master without receiving a dime.

Warranties

The producer declaration agreement also protects the record label against any future legal disputes or copyright infringement cases. The record label needs a warranty that the masters are original and will not infringe on the rights of any third parties.

Music Publishing
("Eat or Die")

"Understanding the music business is understanding music publishing."

I want you to read the following line out loud. *"I WILL STARVE MYSELF TO DEATH IF I DON'T KEEP MY PUBLISHING INCOME."* This is probably the single most important line in this entire book. Music publishing will generate the majority of a producer's income. When I say the majority of a producer's income, I mean about 90 percent! Publishing income comes from record sales, radio and television airplay, movies, video games, ringtones or any possible way that music is enjoyed. The number #1 hit single "Happy" by Pharrell Williams has received top radio airplay, appeared in commercials, film and was nominated for a Grammy and an Oscar. This song has been heard all over the world. Pharrell and his co-writers earn publishing income each time the song was sold, performed and synced to images. To gain a true perspective on how music-publishing works, you need to understand "copyright" which I'll discuss in detail later.

Years ago, a composer or songwriter would need a music "publisher" to print and copy sheet music for distribution into stores for sale to the public. The publisher would then share profits from the sales with the songwriter. Today, music publishers don't act as a "printing company" for songwriters. They help songwriters collect money whenever music is reproduced, performed or sold. Much of the music publishing business lies in the record industry. A music publisher's primary source of income comes from monies received from ASCAP, BMI and SESAC (see Performance Royalty on page 79) and record royalties. If you plan to make a lot of money as a Hip-Hop producer, you also need to be involved in the music publishing business because its the most lucrative and consistent source of income.

Most music producers are also skilled songwriters, both at writing music and lyrics. Typically, Hip-Hop producers don't view themselves as songwriters because of the nontraditional way Hip-Hop music is created. You won't see a Hip-Hop producer sit at a piano and write a hit song. In most cases, you will see a Hip-Hop producer banging away on a Midi or pad controller in front of a computer monitor. The point is, when you create original music, you are in effect creating a "Copyrighted" work or "Copyright." According to Webster's Dictionary, The legal definition of a copyright is *"a limited duration monopoly,"* in other words the *exclusive right*. If you create an original beat or song, you instantly have an "exclusive right" or "copyright" of your original creation.

Producer Prince Paul, known for classic work with Stetsasonic and De La Soul learned a lesson about songwriting early in his career. He says:

> "When we made that song ("Talking All The Jazz" by Stetsasonic) I was really young. I got my friend Newkirk to go and play keyboards on it and I programmed the beats. I look back and I didn't get a writers credit nor did I get production credit on that album, cuz I didn't know, I didn't know a writer meant you could write music as well as lyrics, I thought it was just lyrics."[xxi]

Copyright Ownership

The music industry may look like a complex maze filled with legal obstacles, but it's not that complex if you understand the fundamentals of copyrights. The entire entertainment industry is driven by *six exclusive copyrights* provided by the U.S. government. The concept is simple: *As a creator of an original work, you are given the exclusive rights to perform, distribute, reproduce, display and prepare a derivative of your original.* The six exclusive rights (referred to as "The Big Six") are granted to copyright owners under copyright law. As a Hip-Hop music creator and copyright owner you have the exclusive right to:

THE BEAT GAME

1. **Perform your music**
2. **Distribute your music**
3. **Make copies of your music**
4. **Display your music in public**
5. **Create a derivative of your original work**
6. **Digital Transition**

As you can see, your beats are not just a group of music files sitting on your hard-drive. *They are assets.* It's almost like owning a piece of real estate property that you are able to sell or lease. As a copyright owner, you can grant an individual or company an exclusive right to your music (for a fee of course). The best part about being a copyright owner is that you don't have to grant all of your rights. For example, if someone wants to play your music at a club, you can give them permission to play the music. Under copyright law, there are rules that help govern how copyright owners shall be paid.

When you are "selling beats," you are really transferring your rights or your ownership in your work. The term "selling beats" should have a new meaning to you now. If you thought you can give an A&R representative or artist music on CD in exchange for money and the deal is done, it's not that easy. You will still need to grant the exclusive rights or "copyright" ownership of your original work to the party involved (for them to use your music).

How To Get A Copyright

In theory, when you make a tangible copy of your song, you have a copyright. A tangible copy could be in the form of a video or audiocassette tape, CD, written on paper or any other physical material. United States copyright law gives copyright holders exclusive rights even without a registration with the U.S. copyright office in Washington, D.C. But, that doesn't mean you shouldn't bother with the registration process. Registering your work can be beneficial in the following ways:

1. Gives the owner a certificate of registration.
2. Gives the owner *proof of copyright* on the public record.
3. Makes the new work eligible for statutory damages and attorney's fees in successful litigation.
4. Evidence in a court of law.

Other Ways to Prove Copyright

Other than registering your work with the U.S. copyright office to obtain evidence of copyright, you may do what is called a "poor man's copyright." This is the act of mailing an original copy of your work through the U.S. postal service to receive a postage date. If the package remains unopened the postage date may be used as proof to show the date of origination.

Another form of evidence could be a digital hard drive. Although very costly, you may be able to show proof of a files creation by date through a computer forensic scientist.

Collaborations

As a beat maker or producer, you will be collaborating with many artists, musicians and songwriters to create new music. Much of your financial success will depend on whom you collaborate with, and how the collaboration is formed. As I mentioned above, U.S. Copyright law gives a single copyright owner exclusive rights, but what if a copyright was created by multiple individuals? Let's say as a beat maker, you create the music while another person creates the lyrics for a song. The copyright ownership of the song is "split" between both songwriters and you the music writer. Industry insiders often refer to a percentage of copyright ownership an individual may own or control as "publishing splits."

You may have noticed I didn't say that publishing splits are divided equally. Historically, a song has been divided equally giving 50% to the writer of the music (the beat maker or producer) and 50% going to the lyricist. This may seem like an easy formula to follow but things can quickly get complicated if there isn't a clear definition of what "music" is. In music genres such as country, its not uncommon for the lyricist to create the melody thereby making a "music" contribution to the copyright. In Hip-Hop music, the track and instrumentation in which the lyrics are laid on are considered to be the "music" portion of a song. This information is especially important for beat makers and producers who incorporate samples into its production. The sample owner's publishing's share is usually deducted out of the music share of a song (see "Eating Samples" page 125).

There are no provisions under the U.S. Copyright Act that require a collaborator to gain shares of ownership in a work based on his or her level of contribution. Even if you believe your contribution was essential and an important element to a song, that doesn't necessarily give you the right to the larger percentage of shares in the song. For example, let's assume that a beat maker created the background music (tempo, rhythm, instrumentation, programming, etc) for a song. The beat maker was *inspired* by melodies ideas and lyrics created by the lyric writer. Considering this fact, the lyric writer believes she deserves a 50% share of the *music side of the publishing* because of the "inspiration" she provided. The beat maker totally disagrees with the lyric writer's position. Let's also look at this scenario in reverse. What if a beat maker created the music and wrote lyrics for the chorus of a song? Doesn't the beat maker deserve a percentage of the lyric side of the publishing share too? The differences in ideologies can quickly lead to disputes between collaborators.

As a rule of thumb, beat makers and producers should make a effort to determine each individual publishing split *before* you do any production work. All parties should negotiate the publishing splits based on who contributed what to the particular song at hand. It also should be documented. I heavily endorse negotiations being done as a split sheet (see Illustration 5). There should at least be an informal meeting to hammer out the details. The bottom line: if you don't agree and maintain a sizable publishing split or songwriter's share, you won't be paid anything.

DARRELL "DIGGA" BRANCH

Songwriter Split Sheet

Song Title:_____

Date:_____
(if more than one day, include each day)

Recording Artist:_____Record Label_____
(if any)
Studio Name_____
(recording origin)
Studio Address_____
Studio Phone Number_____
Sample Yes   No (Circle One)   Interpolation Yes No (Circle One)
Sample Contributor_____
(who presented the sample/interpolation)

Song and Artist where Sample originated_____

Composer/Writer 1_____
Affiliation: ASCAP BMI SESAC OTHER (Circle One)

Ownership %: Lyric_____Music:_____(Idenify each % of ownership)

Writer/Composer Signature_____
Social Security#_____Birthday_____

Composer/Writer 2 Information

Composer/Writer 3 Information

Composer/Writer 4 Information

Composer/Writer 5 Information

Composer/Writer 6 Information

Illustration 5.

Once you obtain your publishing split or songwriter's share, you essentially enter into a partnership agreement with other songwriters or shareholders of the copyrighted work. For example, if you own a 50% publishing share and two additional songwriters own the remaining 50%, no individual songwriter or partner can issue any exclusive rights without consent from all partners. So, even if a beat maker or producer creates the entire instrumental background and the songwriters contribute words and lyrics, the beat maker or producer cannot issue any rights to the instrumental portion of the copyrighted work without consent from the songwriters. I know you're thinking, *I did all the music and I deserved to control my 50% share!* Before you take that position, you should understand that there are some benefits to being a partner with a share of the entire copyrighted work.

Real Scenario:

Let's assume that you own a 50% publishing share in a song you produced for Lil Wayne. Let's also assume that Lil Wayne owns the remaining 50% publishing share. Five years after the song is released, another Hip-Hop artist comes along with a new song that contains an interpolation of Lil Wayne's original lyrics. The Hip-Hop artist initiates the sample clearance process and under this scenario, the artist and record label would need permission from Lil Wayne and you, the beat maker. Even though the borrowed elements were influenced by Lil Wayne's lyrics and not derived from the "music" portion of your original song, the 50% share you have in the song allows you to negotiate your own sample clearance arrangement with the Hip-Hop artist or potential user.

Instrumental Copyright Trick

There are ways that beat makers or producers can have their cake and eat it too. It's a rather unorthodox approach to protecting your copyright. With the support of a crafty attorney, a beat maker or producer can keep 100% ownership of all rights associated with their instrumentals while still maintaining the flexibility to collaborate with others. The solution is simple but must be done in several steps.

The first step is to copyright all of your instrumental musical compositions before collaborating with any artist. This is a critical step that shouldn't be overlooked because as you will see later, your initial copyright registrations will provide the foundation needed to structure this kind of deal.

After copyright registration is complete, you are now ready to collaborate with other artist and musicians. Remember, your early copyright registration gives you 100% ownership of the instrumental version of a song. If you collaborate with a songwriter using a copyrighted instrumental, you are effectively creating a derivative of your own work thereby making you the controlling interest in the new work. (See illustration 6 below).

The Beat Maker's Share

Original Track   Derivative Track

100 % Instrumental   50% Vocal
Version   Version

Illustration 6.

The final step in the process is to have your attorney draft an agreement, which guarantees that you maintain 100% ownership of the original instrumental copyright. This may become a huge hurdle to get over during negotiations. The record label will be resistant towards any type of deal that doesn't involve copyright and master recording ownership. Artists and future collaborators may also be reluctant to enter into a deal where ownership is limited to a single version.

You may be asking yourself, *why should I go through all of this?* To maximize your revenue opportunities, that's why! If a major film company wants to place one of your songs in their movie. The "instrumental" version of the song will be part of a dance scene and they are willing to pay $100,000 for the synchronization license. Do you think you should have to fork over $50,000 to the lyric writer even though the vocal version isn't used?

Beat Maker Made For Hire

Being the creator or author of an original copyrighted work doesn't necessarily make you the owner of the copyright. Under copyright law, a *"work made for hire"* is a work specifically prepared by an employee within the scope of his or her employment. In essence, it is perfectly legal to hire a person or group of people with the purpose of creating an original work. Many beat makers have fell victim to the "work made for hire" provision largely because of the lack of knowledge when it comes to copyright law.

Record labels frequently use the "work made for hire" provision to obtain the master recording rights of musical compositions. As I mentioned in the "Producer Declaration" section, it's a fairly common practice for record labels to do everything possible to obtain the master sound recording rights from copyright owners. In the earlier days, record companies owned the recording studios and employed the performing artists, songwriters and musicians, hence making all sound recordings created "works made for hire." Unfortunately, things haven't changed that much. Most record companies still insist on obtaining ownership of all master recordings under "works made for hire" even if the company hasn't technically or officially hired the copyright owner.

Mechanical Income

The Copyright Act of 1976 gives creators (you) exclusive rights to your work. Anyone who wants to distribute your music has to pay what is called a *"mechanical royalty."* As I said earlier, mechanical royalties are monies usually paid by a record company for the right to use your song. The fee in copyright terms is called the statutory rate. A statute in the 1976 Copyright Act sets this rate. Now, what does that mean to you? That means under the law, the record company has to pay you the statutory rate of 9.1 cents per song. The record company must obtain a compulsory mechanical license from the copyright owner, which is you!

Performance Income

How do you get paid when your song is played on the radio?

Well, a representative from each radio station across the globe comes to your home with a payment every time your song is played... If you believe that, then you will believe I also wear a red and white suit and deliver gifts during the holidays. As we discussed earlier, one of your rights as a copyright owner is the "public performance right." No one can play your music on the radio, in nightclubs, bars, concerts, parades, television or any other public place without your permission and consent. According to The Performance Rights Act, commercial radio stations are required to pay a royalty to the musicians that perform on the song the stations play.

A radio station has to get a "performance license" to play your work publicly. *Does every radio station have to get a performance license to play my song?* Absolutely! But instead of you issuing thousands of licenses to radio stations around the world, you can join a Performance Rights Organization to issue licenses for you.

If you read the liner notes in most popular albums, you will probably see at least one of these acronyms, ASCAP, BMI or SESAC. These are the three major *performing rights societies* (also referred to as a P.R.O., Performance Rights Organizations) that represent songwriters and publishers (you). ASCAP stands for American Society of Composers, Authors, and Publishers but most people refer to it as simply, ASCAP (pronounced as-kap). BMI stands for Broadcast Music Incorporated. The last one, SESAC stands for Society of European Stage Authors and Composers. As I mentioned earlier, it's almost physically impossible for you to issue a license to every radio station that plays your music. It's not just your song being played; there are thousands of songs that are being played on the radio as well. These societies make life easier by issuing one big "blanket license" that covers the usage of all the songs controlled by its affiliated songwriters and publishers. In exchange for the blanket license, the radio station pays a fee that ranges in the millions of dollars each year. The fee is then divided up and shared between the songwriters and publishers. A percentage of a 20 million dollar blanket fee seems like some great income right? Don't get too excited though, you won't be getting a share of any fees if your music isn't performed.

Will I get paid if my beat is played one single time on the radio? Possibly. It really depends on which P.R.O. you are a member of and how your beat is being used on the radio. All P.R.O.'s collect blanket license fees that are used to pay songwriters and publishers. Each P.R.O. uses a different payment system and performance scale to determine how much each songwriter and publisher will be paid though. For example, a song being played on the radio 100 times per day will generate a higher payment for a songwriter compared to a song being played half as much. Songwriters in theory earn credit each time their song is played and paid based on the amount of credits they receive during a particular period. Let's dispel the myth right now; P.R.O.'s don't track every play on the radio. Although, it is technically possible to do so in this day and age, most P.R.O.'s continue to use a more conventional method.

BMI uses two methods to track song performances on radio and television: (1) they require several stations to keep a log of all the songs being played during a 3-day period; (2) they also digitally record certain stations.[xxii] With that combined information, BMI makes projections for stations with similar audiences. For example, say Hot 97 radio station is monitored and recorded by BMI. Your song has been recorded over 100 times during the monitoring. Hot 107.5 radio station also logs your song manually over 100 times. BMI will use this information to determine your royalty payout for a specific pay period. Of course there are other factors that have an impact on payouts such as the size of the radio audience, time of day and how long your song was played or performed on the radio.

ASCAP uses a different system. It uses a digital system that conducts census and sample surveys. The census survey is done by doing a complete count of each performance if it's financially feasible to do so. In most cases, they use the sample survey that provides more accurate statistics. To perform this kind of survey, ASCAP records a sample of each radio station from every region of the country, at all times of the day, all days of the year.[xxiii] A station that pays a larger licensing fee may be sampled more than others.

SESAC uses a different system and payment formula altogether. By using technology supplied by BDS (Broadcast Data System), SESAC tracks performances on a census basis on over 14 million hours of radio air time annually. Compared to the other two major P.R.O.'s, SESAC's payment formula is much more simplified. They use the following math equations:

Performances x Affiliate Share x Bonus Factor (where applicable) = Credits

Radio License Fees Available for Distribution / Total Credits = Value Factor

Credits x Value Factor = Royalty Payment[xxiv]

Each P.R.O. has an award system that issues bonus payments to songwriters and publishers whose musical work reaches a certain performance level during a quarterly period. These are sometimes called "The Hit Songs." Bonuses are paid out based on the system of your particular P.R.O. For example, let's say your song receives over 100,000 performances (spins) over a 3-month period. Most P.R.O.'s will pay you an additional bonus percentage for reaching such a milestone. In most cases, the bonuses increase for every benchmark level you reach. For every 50,000 spins, you can increase your royalty payout.

On the flip side, you won't receive much of a performance credit if your song is played a single time on a commercial radio station. Even if you do receive a moderate amount of spins, once all the P.R.O. deducts its fee, your royalty won't amount to much. No matter which P.R.O. you choose, make sure you are satisfied with its payment structure and royalty calculation system. The big three Performing Right Organizations work with composers, songwriters and music publishers to ensure that its affiliates are compensated when their music is publicly performed. Do your research and choose the P.R.O. that works diligently to collect your money and to fulfill all of your professional needs.

SoundExchange

"SoundExchange" is also a performing rights organization, but instead of collecting money for songwriters, it collects money for performers, artists and musicians who perform on recorded songs. For example, a songwriter may compose a song and receive royalties from the big three P.R.O.'s. The singer or musician who performed on the song will receive royalties from SoundExchange. As a copyright owner and performer, you should become a member of SoundExchange to administer the performance rights of your sound recordings. Most beat makers and producers play or perform instruments and vocals on their own tracks. If you do, you have public performance rights under the U.S. copyright law. Forty-five percent of the royalty on each track goes to the main recording artist and 5% to the session musicians and backup singers on that track though RaRoyalties.org. The other 50% of the royalties go to the owner of the master recording, which might be a record label or you, the independent publisher.

Music Publishers

The music publishing industry is one of the most financially lucrative areas of the music business. Unlike artists who are able to generate income by touring and merchandising, a producer's income comes from production and publishing royalties. Record labels aren't the only companies looking for music from producers. Music publishers are looking to work with songwriters and producers on various music projects. While most view the record label as the main avenue for a producer to land a production opportunity, publishing companies also have many great opportunities.

Full Scale Publishing Company

A full-scale publishing company operates much like any corporation that has divisions responsible for handling specific tasks. While some people might refer to full-scale companies as "major" publishers, I refrain from using that reference because it suggests that any other publishing entity is "low level" or some equivalent. All publishing companies operate in much the same way but full-scale companies are usually fully staffed. Some full-scale companies have song catalogs of more than 500,000 copyrights.

Independent Publishers

An independent publisher is any individual, company or firm NOT affiliated with a major record label. Most independent record labels also operate their own publishing division to manage its copyright catalog. There are a variety of independent publishers that represent prominent songwriters with sizable catalogues. For example, Downtown Music Publishing, established in 2007 has a catalog, which has grown to include over 40,000 copyrights. Downtown represents myself and writers who have penned hit singles for artists such as Bruno Mars, Carrie Underwood to name a few. If you decide to start your own publishing company, you will be the owner of your own "independent" publishing company.

Record Company Affiliates

Most record labels or record companies of any size own or work closely with a publishing company partner. Some label-affiliated publishers function "independently" of its parent company or partner. Most record companies set up departments or divisions that are responsible for administering copyrights which are owned, partly owned or controlled by recording artist affiliated with the record label. The four major music distributors all have full-scale affiliated publishing companies. Warner Music Group publishing arm Warner/Chappell Music administers a catalog of more than one million copyrights from songwriters such as Katy Perry, Lil Wayne, Timbaland, T.I. and others. Universal Music Group's publishing division is arguably the leader in music publishing in the U.S. representing songwriters like U2, Elton John, Eminem, producer Hit-Boy and more. At the time of this writing, Sony Music Entertainment and its publishing arm Sony/ATV is in the process of acquiring EMI Music Publishing (publishing affiliate of major distributor EMI Music) effectively making three major publishing affiliates instead of four. With this merger, Sony will control the largest number of copyrights in the music business-more than 2 million. Sony/ATV will also have a diverse catalogue of songs written by artist such as Beyonce, Rihanna, Bob Dylan, Michael Jackson and other legendary artists.

Producer - Owned Companies

Setting up your own publishing company should be the first thing that all beat makers and producers do. Most "superstar" producers own full-scale publishing companies that sign additional songwriters, manage catalogs and pitch music for use in television and film. For example, legendary producer Dr. Dre also runs a publishing company that represents a variety of songwriters, musicians, beat makers and producers. The late Michael Jackson made a large portion of his fortune by income he received from owning ATV publishing. Before his death, he joined forces with Sony Music to form Sony/ATV music publishing. Today, the company is one of the largest publishers in music with catalogs from The Beatles and Michael Jackson himself.

Publishing Deals

A publishing deal is by far the most important deal a beat maker or producer can enter into. Publishing is the number one revenue source for beat makers and producers. So, it's very important that you understand what type of deal may be right or very WRONG for you. Other than the production or management deal, the publishing deal is the most substantial and lucrative deal in most cases. If you plan to sign a music publishing deal, I strongly advise that you consult with an experienced attorney before entering into any type of agreement. There are various types of publishing deals that can be structured to benefit beat makers financially without losing 100% ownership in their music. Let's take a look the basic deals:

Administration Deals

An administration deal is a great deal for beat makers or producers looking to maintain 100% ownership in their copyright catalog. Under an administration (sometimes referred to as an "admin" deal), you can keep full ownership of all your songs and grant rights to an "administrator" (typically a larger publishing company) to take on certain responsibilities. These responsibilities include song licensing, copyright registration, royalty collection, song pitching and more. The administrator receives a fee usually in the range of 10% to 25% of the gross revenue. All administration deals aren't created equal though. You don't have to relinquish all of your exclusive rights to a single administrator. Although it may cause confusion for potential users, you can assign administration rights to multiple administrators. The most common administration arrangement is with one administrator who is granted all exclusive rights but as you may see later, this can cause some additional issues for you. (See the illustration 7).

Administration Deals
(Beat Maker Retains 100% Ownership In All Copyrights)

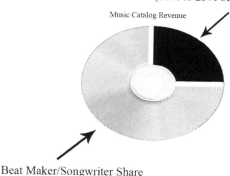

Administrator Share
(10% to 25% of gross revenue)

Music Catalog Revenue

Beat Maker/Songwriter Share
(75% to 90% of gross revenue)

Illustration 7.

Standard Publishing Deals

A standard or "traditional" publishing deal is usually an agreement where both parties agree to split all publishing revenue from songs generated under the terms of the deal (and sometimes after the deal). Under this agreement, the beat maker or producer will transfer 50% ownership in it's copyright in exchange for an advance payment. In theory, the publisher will own a 50% share in all copyrighted songs created under the terms of the deal. Beat makers and producers can negotiate lucrative deals with huge advances for 50% of ownership in your catalogue. The publisher's position is, "I can pay the beat maker $50,000 for 50% ownership in his or her songs for the next 5 years." The beat makers position is usually, "I can receive a $50,000 advance right now without waiting for my songs to generate income." This will be the dilemma you will be faced with in this type of deal. (See illustration 8 below).

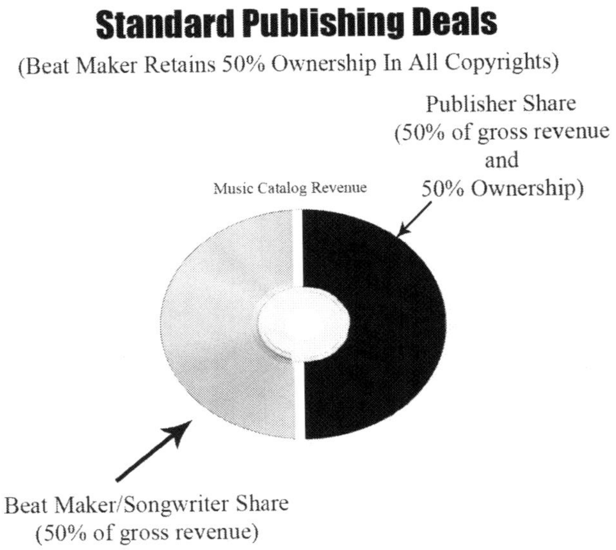

Standard Publishing Deals

(Beat Maker Retains 50% Ownership In All Copyrights)

Publisher Share
(50% of gross revenue
and
50% Ownership)

Music Catalog Revenue

Beat Maker/Songwriter Share
(50% of gross revenue)

Illustration 8.

Co-Publishing Deals

A co-publishing deal is structured more like a partnership agreement between the beat maker or producer and publishing company. Under a co-publishing deal, a beat maker or producer agrees to transfer a percentage of its *publishing share* (usually 50%) to a publisher or publishing company. This is where the numbers get a bit tricky. Now, in a standard publishing deal the beat maker transfers 50% ownership in the entire copyright, which is also 100% of the publishing share. In a co-publishing deal, the beat maker will transfer 25% ownership in the copyright and 50% of the publishing share. The co-publishing deal ends up being split 75/25 with the beat maker receiving a 75% share of everything when you factor in the writer's share (50% writer's share +25% publisher's share =75% beat maker's share). The publishing share is divided by 50% but NOT your writer's share. So, actually you are only giving up 25% of your publishing income (50% of publishing share) while retaining 100% of your writer's share.

Most publishers also perform administrative duties for a fee, of course. As I mentioned earlier, the administration fee ranges from 10% to 25% in standard and co-publishing deals. The administration fee is deducted from the gross publishing income before any deductions are made. For example, if the administration fee were 10%, the beat maker/songwriter and publisher would divide the reminding 90%. Or the beat maker/songwriter would receive a 75% share and the publisher would receive a 25% share. (See illustration 9.) .

Co-Publishing Deals
(Beat Maker Retains 75% Ownership In All Copyrights)

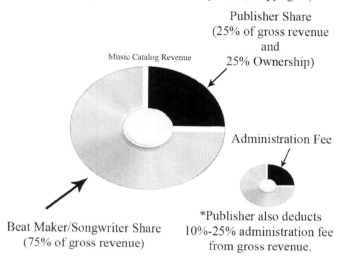

Publisher Share
(25% of gross revenue
and
25% Ownership)

Music Catalog Revenue

Administration Fee

Beat Maker/Songwriter Share
(75% of gross revenue)

*Publisher also deducts
10%-25% administration fee
from gross revenue.

Illustration 9.

Third Party Publishing Deals

A third party publishing deal is an agreement between two or more parties. As you may imagine, things can get complicated when you have multiple parties involved. To get a full understanding of how this deal works, let's identify the three parties involved in this scenario:

6. Beat maker or Producer (copyright owner)
7. Publishing Company One (Full-scale)
8. Publishing Company Two (Independent)

Music publishing deals are typically structured to allow an independent publisher or publishing company to earn a percentage of publishing revenues generated by the public use of works/songs created by the beat maker and producer. But what if an independent publishing company agrees to a partnership deal with a larger or full-scale music publishing company? *Wouldn't that have a financial affect the beat maker or producer?* The answer is yes and unfortunately, the beat maker or producer will end up being affected tremendously under this type of deal. These types of publishing deals are not uncommon and are detrimental to a beat maker or producer's career. Unfortunately, I even became a victim and had to learned the hard way by being tied up in a third party publishing deal early on in my career. See illustration 10 below.

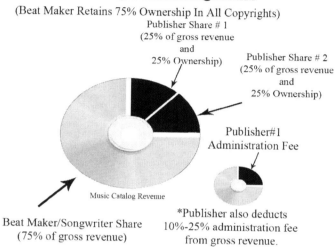

Third Party Publishing Deals
(Beat Maker Retains 75% Ownership In All Copyrights)
Publisher Share # 1
(25% of gross revenue
and
25% Ownership)

Publisher Share # 2
(25% of gross revenue
and
25% Ownership)

Publisher#1
Administration Fee

Music Catalog Revenue

Beat Maker/Songwriter Share
(75% of gross revenue)

*Publisher also deducts
10%-25% administration fee
from gross revenue.

Illustration 10.

To truly understand the dangers and pitfalls you can come across in a third party deal, you really need to play close attention to the percentages. Let's look at some examples:

Example #1

You enter into a co-publishing agreement with Joe Blow Music publishing. As a beat maker (songwriter), you agree to split all publishing revenues 50/50 with Joe Blow Music publishing. Unbeknownst to you at the time, Joe Blow Music agrees to a co-publishing deal with major publisher EMI music publishing. Under the deal, EMI music publishing will be instructed to collect all publishing income on Joe Blow's behalf (which includes revenue from your catalog of songs too). Since EMI receives a percentage from all publishing revenue collected, how much will the beat maker receive in royalties? Let's look at the math:

EMI Music Publishing receives $1.00
-Administration Fee 10%

($1.00 -$.10) Total $.90
-100% Joe Blow Writer's Shares $.45
-50% Joe Blow Publishing Share $.22
-50% EMI Publishing share $.22

Joe Blow Total Publishing Share-$.67
-10% Joe Blow Administration Fee -$.6
-100% Beat Maker Writer's Share $.31
-50 % Joe Blow Publishing share $.15
-50 % Beat Maker's Publishing Share $.15

Total Beat Maker's Share $.46

Example of "Joe Blow Deal"

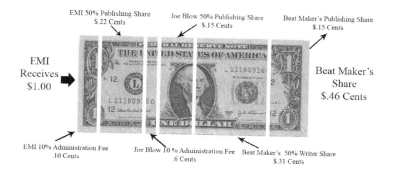

If you were paying close attention, you may have noticed that the total royalty share of the Beat Maker is significantly decreased by $.31 cents because of EMI's 10% administrative fee, Joe Blow's 10% administrative fee and 50% publishing share. Under this deal, you as the beat maker will miss out on .21 cents. That's almost a 50% percentage deduction in your revenue. If a song generated $1 million dollars in revenue, you would stand to lose out on $210,000 in revenue! Let's look at the math without EMI:

Joe Blow Music Publishing receives $1.00

-Administration Fee 10%

($1.00 -$.10) Total $.90

-50% Beat Maker Writer's Share $.45

-50% Beat Maker Publishing Share $.22

-50% Joe Blow Publishing share $.22

Total Beat Maker's Share $.67

And it gets even worse. Until now, I've focused on publishing royalty percentages and how they are divided amongst the beat maker and publisher. This scenario can drastically change when we factor in advanced payments, which are also recoupable against future royalties.

Example #2

Let's say you produced a hit song that generates over $100,000 in publishing income. You received an advance of $50,000 at the initial signing of your publishing deal with Joe Blow Music. After recouping your advance, you are owed $50,000. Now, Joe Blow has also received a $100,000 advance from EMI music publishing at the initial signing of their partnership deal. Under this scenario, the $100,000 in publishing income generated by your songs will be credited towards the recoupment of the $100,000 advanced paid to Joe Blow Music by EMI music publishing. So, even though your song has earned $100,000 and effectively recouped your $50,000 advance according to your publishing deal, Joe Blow will owe you money but may be unable to pay you until the $100,000 advance from EMI is recouped. Joe Blow may be able to pay royalties only if it keeps a reserve fund for this purpose. As a beat maker, you don't want to put yourself in a position to be owed money by a publisher who can't pay you. These numbers are quite modest. Real life publishing advances can range from a few hundred thousand to several million dollars.

The Main Deal Points

A *provision* (also referred to as a *deal point*) is a section in a written agreement that provides specific details for a contingency plan in each area of the deal. Although there are different types of publishing deals, most deals contain similar provisions if they are properly drafted. These provisions are the key areas or deal points that you need to pay special attention to during negotiations. You definitely need a qualified attorney to review any contract agreement but you also need to be educated enough to read it over yourself. Some of the language or legal jargon might be a little intimidating to comprehend at first but as you become familiar with reading agreements, you will develop an understanding. Lets go over each provision point one by one:

Grant of Rights

This provision lays out in detail what rights you will be granting to the publisher. Each point within this section (often formatted in bullets) will describe how the publisher will use each right assigned to them. For example, the first right granted would be: to perform and license others to perform the music publicity or privately, for profit or otherwise, by means of public or private performance, radio broadcast, television, or by any other means or media, whether now or conceived or developed later.

Administration

Almost all publishing deals require you to give up specific rights in exchange for a financial advance against future royalties. This deal point gives the music publisher the right to control and exploit the music.

An effective music publisher will do this by issuing mechanical, synchronization and performance licenses. A publisher may also need permission from you to collect money from the rights that are granted to third parties. For example, you may have an international music publisher who has the administration rights to your music outside of the United States. The "administration" fee charged by the publisher is usually about 10% but I've heard of fees being as much as 25% of the gross publisher's share of income.

Minimum Delivery Release Commitment

This provision requires a beat maker or producer to deliver a minimum amount of original copyrighted works to the music publisher or publishing company. For example, a publisher may require a beat maker to deliver a minimum of 3 original songs (or a collection of song shares totaling 300%) to fulfill specific terms of the agreement. This gives a publisher the minimum amount of copyrights needed to generate royalties to recoup advance payments.

Royalties

This provision describes in detail how royalties are split between the writer (you) and publisher. Other than the "Grant of Rights" provision, the royalty provision is the most important deal point. Under a typically "co-publishing deal, there is usually a 50/50 split between the copyright owner and publisher. The publisher gets 50% of the publishing share with the writer maintaining 100% of the writer's share. So in reality, the writer receives 75% of all income. In an administration deal, the royalties are split with 85% going to the writer and 15% going to the administrator/publisher. Make sure your royalties are calculated from "the source" based on the gross income. The publisher should never make any deductions before determining the percentage splits. As a song writer and/or beat maker, always negotiate an "at source" deal to maximize your income.

Term

This provision sets the period in which the agreement will be in effect. Most publishing agreements includes terms that are based on a combination of calendar years and the *minimum delivery commitment*. For example, the terms of the agreement may be for one year or until a specified number of copyrighted songs have been delivered to the publisher.

Option Period

An option period is the time in which an option can be exercised. Option periods are used to extend the term of the agreement. It usually occurs before or on the expiration date the initial agreement was completed. When the initial term of the agreement ends, an option period (usually the publisher's option) may begin. Make sure you pay close attention to when the option period begins and ends. Most option periods require the publisher to make an additional advance payment to you (recoupable against royalties of course).

Licensing of Masters

This provision gives the publisher the authority to issue a master license for each master recording under the terms of the agreement. Publishers can only issue licenses for master recordings they own or control. Remember, the "master" is the copyrighted work *embodied* in a multitrack tape or digital file and not who possesses the actual tapes or digital file the song is recorded on.

Accounting

The accounting provision lays out in detail how the publisher will be handling the book keeping process. For example, the publisher may designate specific dates in which they may notify you about payments and statements. In most cases, you can expect to receive a statement every 6 months (usually in April and October). This provision also describes how the auditing process will be conducted. If there is issues with receiving the full amount owed to you, this provision provides a procedure that will be fair to all parties involved.

Warranties and Indemnifications

This provision is added to protect all parties if there is a dispute. The publishing or record company will need a guarantee from you that any songs created under the agreement are free and clear of any copyright claims. Each company will try it's hardest to add language in a contract that protects them against infringement lawsuits. An indemnification is the act of making another party whole by paying for any loss another party might suffer. For example, if a lawsuit arises, the publishing company may require you to pay their attorney fees or any other financial losses.

Controlled Composition Clause

Now that you have a good understanding of how mechanical licensing works, let's discuss how it might NOT work out for you. A controlled composition is a song written, owned or controlled by a *recording artist.* The "Controlled Composition" clause is a section in an agreement usually between the "record label," "artist" and "producer." This clause is very important to record labels that look to limit the amount of mechanical royalties it will be obligated to pay the artist and the "producer" too! Remember, the producer and artist are often tied together in everything. So, if a recording artist agrees to certain stipulations in the controlled composition clause, it could have negative implications on the producer's mechanical income as well. Remember, a record label must pay out mechanical royalty payments to the copyright owner or songwriter but that doesn't stop a record label from trying to negotiate with you to pay a lower rate. Record labels are unable to use your mechanical income as a way to recoup advances, recording costs, or any other expenses connected to a recording artist and producer.

As I stated earlier, the U.S. statutory mechanical rate is 9.1 cents for songs 5 minutes or less. The record labels have found creative ways to insert language into contracts that get them out of paying the entire 9.1 cents per song. For example, if an average album has a 12-song track list, we can calculate the total mechanical rate for the entire album. It's 9.1 cents multiplied by 12 songs totaling a little more than $1.09 per album. *Do you think record companies want to pay out $1.09 per album?* Nope!

Did I mention that the record label can't recoup these fees from you either? Remember, these are not production royalties.

Now, using the example from above you might say to yourself *"all I have to do is sell a few hundred thousand records and I'm rich!"* Not so fast. Remember, the record label doesn't want to pay the entire $1.09 and they have a few ways to get around it. One is by adding a *controlled composition clause* in recording agreements with artists. Many provisions inside an artist recording agreement affect the producer as well. The controlled composition clause sets a limit on how many songs the record label will pay the artist for. For example, the record label may ask the artist to reduce his or her statutory rate 25% for each song. If he or she agrees to the lower rate, your rate can be reduced too! You may be saying to yourself, *I won't agree to have my rate lowered because of someone else. That shouldn't affect me!* If you weren't paying attention, it will definitely affect you and your pockets too.

As an up-and-coming producer, it will become very challenging to negotiate with an artist and record label especially pertaining to the controlled composition clause. This will clearly be an area where the artist and record label will attempt to take advantage. If a recording artist has a controlled composition clause in their recording agreement with the record label, chances are he or she will ask you to also accept a similar arrangement in your production agreement. For example, if an artist agrees to lower their mechanical rate to 7 cents per song, you may be asked to adjust your rate to reflect the same deduction. Instead of receiving a mechanical rate of 4.5 cents, your rate would be reduced to 3.5 cents. One cent may not seem like much money, but it's a 25% reduction in your royalty rate. If the song generates $1 million dollars in income, you would be losing out on nearly $250,000! As you become more successful, you will be able to negotiate a more favorable mechanical royalty rate.

My personal experience in the world of the "controlled composition" clause came when I produced a song for rapper/entrepreneur, Jay Z. My attorney received what seemed to be a fairly standard producer agreement from Jay Z's attorney. After further review, my attorney informed me that there was a controlled composition clause and that Jay Z would like me to accept a lower mechanical rate. Agreeing to accept a lower mechanical royalty rate wasn't much of a big deal because realistically the deduction amounted to what I thought would've been a fraction of a penny. I agreed to be paid *BASED on all controlled compositions* proved to be a huge mistake. Because I agreed to be "tied" to the composition clause, I essentially agreed to a prorated mechanical royalty too. It gets worse: because of the multiple usages of samples on the album, the mechanical royalty pot was dramatically decreased. Remember, sample owners usually want the maximum statutory rate and are not subject to any cap or control composition clause. The sample owners take all there money off the top and everyone else is left to split the balance of the pot. In the end, all the songwriters including Jay Z had to be paid from a very small pot. Although Jay Z agreed to have his compositions controlled by the record label, he was able to benefit by being a part owner of the record label as well. Remember, record labels don't want to pay mechanical royalties and from Jay Z's perspective, that was good business. Jay Z's strategy was to tie all songwriters to a low controlled composition cap. This allowed Jay Z as a co-owner, to limit royalty payouts and retain more profits for his record label.

Setting Up A Publishing Company

Read closely: *Setting up your own publishing company is the first thing you should do after reading this section.* This should be the first business entity created by you even before your "Production" entity. Like we discussed earlier, publishing income is derived from the exploitation of your music. The first thing you need to do is affiliate your "company-to-be" with a performance rights organization such as ASCAP, BMI or SESAC.

Setting Up A Publishing Company Instructions

Each P.R.O. has its own registration process but you can use these instructions to help guide you along the way. Remember that you will need to know some basic information about yourself such as your legal name, social security number, date of birth and have a tentative name for your publishing company.

Let's go over this step by step:

1. *If you are reading this, you're off to a great start.* You need to do research and educate yourself on business management and music publishing. Books about management and music are available at the public library, bookstores and online. The Internet is also a great source to find information for free.

2. *Before you can start your own publishing company, you need to own and control your copyrights.* We can assume that the first copyright you will intend to publish will be your own. When you get set-up and gain the confidence of other writers, you will need to retain a lawyer to assist you in drafting agreements between your "publishing company" and writers.

3. *Choose at least three names you would like to use for your publishing company.* This will be the name that will be registered with your county clerk's office and with your performance rights organization. Contact your local county clerk's office and search the records to see if your name choice is in use. This is why it's extremely important to choose three unique names because your first choice could be previously registered. Registering a name with the county clerk's office allows the public to know that you will be "Doing Business As," using a name other than your full legal name. For example, the county records for my publishing company states "Darrell Branch DBA Figga Six Music Publishing Company (DBA is an acronym for "doing business as").

4. *Become an affiliate of a performing rights organization such as ASCAP, BMI or SESAC.* The process is very simple. As I stated earlier, you should choose a unique name that can be registered with the county clerk and your P.R.O. Each society gives you the opportunity to choose a unique name for your publishing company. The application will ask you to provide

your name, date of birth, social security, address and genre of music.

5. ***Open a business bank account using your new business name.*** Remember, this is your account for all business transactions and should never be combined with your personal funds. Combining business and personal accounts or using funds from the business account may create problems with accounting and tax matters for you later on.

The Harry Fox Agency

The Harry Fox Agency works closely with music publishers to collect mechanical and digital licensing income from users. It acts as an agent for music publishers who issue mechanical and digital licenses to record manufacturers and distributors. By affiliating with HFA, publishers have access to a range of licensing, collection, distribution, royalty compliance and legal services to assist them in administrating their catalog. Because of its large roster of publisher affiliates, users and licensees are able to complete their mechanical licenses through HFA. As an independent publisher, you need to become an affiliate of HFA to act as your agent for issuing mechanical licenses and collecting royalties. Find out more at: https://www.harryfox.com/public/Licensee.jsp

Sampling

Sampling is a technique in which the foundation of Hip-Hop music originated. Sampling is much more than borrowing music from the past. The use of sampled elements adds texture and depth when combined with one another. Sampling a drum section from a James Brown song and combining it with a Jimi Hendrix guitar riff creates something new and unique. Sampling gives a beat maker the ability to fuse sounds from the past with current music trends. One could incorporate prerecorded musical elements from musicians who might not normally collaborate with one another. Hip-Hop beat makers have taken sampling technology to new heights. That's what makes our craft great and continue to thrive. Hip Hop can transcend cultural boundaries.

Chopping Samples

Chopping samples is a technique used by beat makers to slice, edit and rearrange elements usually taken from a prerecorded song. This is done with some form of a digital editor either in a hardware instrument such as a digital sampler or using a computer-based software program. The concept behind "chopping" a sample was derived from the need to divide it into individual sections or sounds. Once the sample is sliced into individual pieces, each sound can then be modified in various ways. For example, let's say you have a re-recorded piano piece. Chopping the sample will allow you to split the piano piece into various parts thereby giving you the ability to rearrange, extend, copy, pitch, layer and change the volume of each individual sample part.

Developing the skill to chop samples take much more than just randomly selecting a sample to trim into individual parts. It takes creativity, technical skill and most importantly a vision to imagine the possibilities of what a sample can add to your production. Much of the skill of chopping starts with learning how to listen. I developed the skill of chopping through a lot of trial and error. There is no "right" or "wrong" way to chop and flip samples as long as your are achieving the sound you desire. Studying and listening to beats created by sampling greats such as J Dilla, Pete Rock and DJ Premier helped me a great deal. The most important element in my self-development came from simply experimenting. I would start by recording a drum sequence first to establish a *groove*. Then, I would play around with all sorts of sample chops (individual sounds) over the drum sequence until I developed something that sounded good. This strategy still works for me today.

Music producer and YouTube phenomenon Donnie "Boon Doc" Mayfield gave me his take on chopping samples:

> I can tell if a producer needs to improve on their sample chopping skills in many ways. When they don't know their measures in music and are chopping pieces too early or too late from the 1 count. When the grooves are off, the sample will have this really swinging groove, but they lay it over drums with no swing at all. If they're slicing, and you can hear all the spaces in between the pads they're hitting. Also, when they don't arrange the samples accordingly with how music works. If your familiar with music theory, and you should be, you would know that you never use dissonant chords or passing chords as your main chord. It will sound unsettling. The sample might be doing just a simple I and IV chord progression, but has a dissonant passing chord just before it goes back to the I. And some cat will chop that passing tone, and play it like the main chord. It just won't make sense, it won't sound right. Like I said, it's all about the ear and just understanding music and how it flows.[xxv]

Chopping samples is much more than a sampling technique to incorporate previously recorded material. The key to all sampling is taking something new or old and turning it into something that's yours. The limited sampling features of electronic samplers like the EMU SP-1200 and the AKAI MPC 60 created an entire community of skilled sample choppers. Some of the most well known Hip-Hop producers have developed successful music careers specifically from the use of the sampling-chopping technique. Legendary producer J-Dilla is widely known as the "Chop King." His ability to take bits and pieces of a song and transform it into a new full-length composition has inspired a generation of beat makers and producers all around the world.

Hungry? Try Eating A Sample

Incorporating samples into your music production has its creative advantages but it can also be a financial nightmare. By using samples, you sacrifice giving up ownership of your copyright and future earnings. Early in my career, an attorney once told me to *"only sample if you really believe the track will be a hit single."* At the time I didn't understand the strategy behind that concept. Today, I understand that songs containing samples need huge record sales and extensive airplay to generate a sizeable income. Even with a small ownership share, a song containing a sample would generate some revenue for a beat maker. On the other hand, if you lack ownership, it's quite possible that you can produce a hit song and not make a dime.

When I was a young kid, I use to love a strawberry cake with lemon frosting. I got so excited around the time of my birthday because I knew my mother would get me my favorite cake for my birthday party. The one thing that made me so upset was when everyone who attended my party would leave the party with a piece of my cake. It was my cake but everyone seemed to enjoy it more than I did. I'm using this birthday cake analogy to show exactly what happens when you incorporate samples into your production. Everyone is happy when the song becomes a huge hit but who will be reaping all the benefits from its success?

Everyone enjoys your birthday party but the question is who will be taking a slice of your cake home with them? Once you add a single sample, you are inviting songwriters, publishers or copyright holders to your party for a slice of cake. People who have been sampled become instant collaborators without stepping a foot inside a studio. They may gain a stream of revenue off of a generation of music they don't even listen to or enjoy.

Being a copyright owner has its perks especially when you own an extensive catalog of songs. If you ever attended an ASCAP or BMI Urban Music Awards show, you've probably seen some seventy-year-old songwriter win an award for writing a Hip-Hop song. *How is that possible*, you ask? Because the song contained a sample originally written by that seventy year old. *What a life.* This is why it's extremely important to own your music! Funk singer Rick James bought a huge home with proceeds from MC Hammer's sampled song "You Can't Touch This."

If you decide to use a sample, it won't be the end of the world. You can make money but only if you can hold onto a share of ownership in the copyright. A hit song can generate a few hundred thousand dollars at a minimum in revenue, but if you "eat the sample," you may not receive any money. Eating the sample is another way of saying, "forfeiting a percentage of your share" of ownership. As we discussed earlier, an original composition is usually split equally with a 50% share going to the music writer and a 50% share going to the lyric writer. When a sample is used, which share will the sample owner's percentage come from? You guessed it; the samples percentage is usually taken from the music writer or producer's share. So, in most cases, the producer has to "eat the sample" because the *music side* of the composition contains the sample and not the *writer or lyric side* of the composition (lyrics can contain an interpolation, see page 129). I don't agree with this practice because I believe great musical elements and melodies inspire songwriters to write great lyrics. Thus, if a sample is part of musical elements, the producer shouldn't be penalized for providing inspiration for the songwriter as well.

With a proven track record, you'll be able to negotiate with record labels and their artist to do what is referred to as *"taking the sample off the top."* With the sample coming off the top, the record label and/or artist agree to split the ownership share 50/50 with the producer ONLY after the sample owner has received its ownership share. For example, if a sample owner grants permission in exchange for a 50% ownership share of the new composition, the lyric writer would receive a 25% share and the producer would receive a 25% share. If you (the beat maker) has to "eat the sample" in this scenario, you wouldn't receive anything. Your entire 50% share would be given to the sample owner.

This is a common scenario for Hip-Hop producers. It's not

unusual for a producer to lose out on a substantial amount of income because of the use of samples. In 2004, I produced a song called "Many Men" by 50 cent. It is the highest selling song of my production career selling over 11 Million albums worldwide. Although the song was a major success, I didn't earn as much money as one would think. After all the ownership shares were split, I ended up with only a 10% share. This was because the sample owner demanded a sizable share of the copyright. Don't feel sorry for me though, a 10% share on a song that sold over 11 million copies is nothing to sneeze at.

Real Life Situation #1

Producer Buckwild was in a similar situation with 50 Cent too. He produced a song that appeared on 50 Cent's *Before I Self-Destruct, LP*. The track contained a sample from a song that was in public domain. Normally, this would be good news considering the fact that a song in the public domain is free to use by anyone. The rules change slightly change when sampled elements are from a song in the public domain though. Although public domain copyrights are free to use, the *master recordings* of those copyright are NOT always free to use. Remember, to clear a sample, the user needs permission from the publisher and the owner of the original master recording. In Buckwild's case, he didn't need permission from the publisher because the copyright was in the public domain. He did however need permission from the owner of the master recording and that ironically, was Civil Rights leader Reverend Jessie Jackson.

To obtain permission to clear usage of the master recording, Reverend Jackson and his company wanted 40% ownership in the new copyright (50 Cent & Buckwild's Song) along with a whopping $20,000 advance payment against future royalties. After negotiating for over a month, Buckwild and 50 Cent battled unsuccessfully to lower the proposed fees presented by Jackson's representation. The 40% ownership split and $20,000 fee was paid, along with the remaining 60% being split equally by Buckwild and 50 Cent.

Real Life Situation # 2

While pitching some newly created tracks in early 2004, one track in particular ended up in the hands of a well-known Hip-Hop artist signed to a major record label. He was also well known for his creative approach at incorporating various samples and interpolations into his music. After about a four-month period, I received a call from an A&R notifying me that the artist had selected a track to appear on his upcoming album. Excited and happy about the good news, I immediately went down to the A&R's office to hear the final product. When he played the song, everything sounded great until it got to the chorus. To my disappointment, the artist recited a chorus with a very familiar melody line borrowed from a song released during the 1980s. At this point, I'm thinking: *Did he really need to add that melody? Is he going to have to pay for that?*

What started out as a minor issue, ballooned into a yearlong dispute between the artist and I over shares of song ownership. Under normal circumstances, I would receive a 50% ownership share in the song because I created 100% of the music. The artist or lyric writer would receive a 50% ownership share in the song because they created 100% of the lyrics. This is a simple formula to follow. In my situation, the artist didn't "exactly" create lyrics that were 100% original. His words were original but the cadence in which he performed a few words during the chorus section was not original. As I stated earlier, the chorus borrowed a very familiar melody line from another song. As a result, we needed permission from the copyright owner of the borrowed song. This is where the situation got a bit ugly.

In exchange for being granted permission to use the melody line, the copyright owner of the "borrowed" song wanted a 30% share in our new composition. My first thought was pure shock because I thought the proposed 30% share was way too high for such a minimal usage. However, there wasn't a standard formula to determine the true value of a word, lyric or melody line in a song. The freedom to "name your price" is one of the benefits of being a copyright owner. No one can put a value on your music but you anyway. As a copyright owner, you can determine the value regarding any song derived from your original song.

Sample Replays & Interpolations

Since the very beginning, Hip-Hop music has always been heavily influenced by other genres of music. Even before the first Hip-Hop recording "Rapper's Delight" by the Sugar hill Gang was released, Deejay's use to play the section of songs that featured a solo drum instrumentation referred to as the "break." So, the idea of incorporating certain melodies or lyrics from another song to make a new Hip-Hop record isn't anything new. Over the years, technology has made this process easier to perform with the invention of electronic music equipment samplers and digital software programs. You can sample parts of an original song and manipulate the audio various ways. Most Hip-Hop production is built from sampling an original master recording embodied in vinyl, tape, CD or MP3. But what if you don't "sample" from a copy of an original master? What if you listen to an original master and "replay" it with your own instruments? As I mentioned earlier, some of the first Hip-Hop records did not contain a "sample" but rather what's called an *interpolation*.

A sample interpolation is the act of "changing" or "inserting" something different into an original work. For example, if a band replays the song "Born In The USA" by Bruce Springsteen with their own unique changes, they are creating an "interpolation" of the original version. When you replay an original song without making changes, this is known as a "cover." No permission from the copyright owner is required to replay a song. The production behind the song "Rapper's Delight" by The Sugar Hill Gang is an interpolation of an original song called "Good Times" by Chic. In the earlier days, Hip-Hop producers would bring in musicians to replay or recreate music from original songs. Although it might seem less convenient to work with musicians instead of directly sampling, this was a major benefit for producers at the time.

Typically, when you "clear" a sample, you are being granted permission from both, the owner of the composition and the owner of the master recording the composition is embodied in. The owner of the composition, usually the publisher or publishing company has the control to administer publishing rights. The owner of the master (typically the record label or publishing company) can grant you the right to use the master recording (the record medium you sampled from example. Vinyl, CD, etc.). If you don't sample from a master recording embodying a composition, then you only need to contact the music publisher. This allows you to deal directly with the music publisher or copyright holder. This is also a benefit to you when the copyright owner is not the master owner. I've heard of plenty of cases where the music publisher granted permission but then permission was denied by the master owner. As you might imagine, this creates a horrible predicament for a beat maker and artist to be in, especially if a song has the potential to become a huge hit. Some companies who control the rights of master recordings go overboard and demand exorbitant usage fees. Clearing a sample may be a huge hurdle to get over but creating an interpolation is an alternative, which may cause less of a headache.

The Secret of "The Remix"

Now that you have a basic understanding of copyright law, this is a good time to let you in on the secret of "the remix." Sean "Diddy" Combs said he invented "the remix." You may have also heard producers scream out "REMIX" at the beginning of songs (yet another cliché in urban music). When we hear the word "remix," we commonly think of a music track being rearranged or altered. Despite the common perception, most remix work isn't audible to the average music listener. Most "mixing" is typically done by a "mixer" or "mix engineer" whose main job is to enhance multitrack elements using studio equipment such as audio processors, equalizers and other electrical units. The final product is often referred to as the "mix".

A "remix" is an alternative version of a recorded song derived from an original version. So, by definition, any added elements and alterations made to an original version of a song could be classified as a "remix."

Until this point, we have spent a considerable amount of time covering your rights pertaining to the "original recording" or "original song." What about your rights to an alternative version of a song? What if you create a dance remix for a single, do you have rights? What if someone else creates a pop remix derived from your original song?

Can't Stop, Won't Stop?

In 2003, I produced a song named "Can't Stop, Won't Stop" featuring Roc-a-fella Records recording artist Young Gunz. The song became a major hit reaching as high as #14 on the billboard hot 100 charts along with being nominated for a Grammy the following year. To continue to build on the song's success, Roc-a-fella Records decided to commission me to do a remix version of the song. However, this version would feature a guest appearance by a major recording artist. This is a common strategy used by record labels that want to extend the performance life of a hit song. Adding a featured artist to a remix usually pumps new energy into a hit song. This enables the song to continue to gain radio and television airplay, thereby increasing record sales.

Young Gunz decided to collaborate and feature Saint Louis rapper Chingy. At the time, Chingy was also topping the music charts with his single "Right Thurr." After the remix was complete, I was notified through my publishing company that Chingy and his publishing company wanted a percentage of ownership in the "remix" version of "Can't Stop, Won't Stop." Because the remix was a derivative work of the original song, Chingy was not entitled to ownership. This didn't stop him and his publishers from pushing to get it. In situations such as this, the featured artist is usually paid a one-time fee to appear on the remix and in the promotional video if applicable. Chingy wanted more and even threatened not to show up for the video shoot. After weeks of negotiation, Young Gunz and I agreed to register the remix as a new work. This enabled Chingy to get an ownership share, but only in the "remix" version. I only agreed to give up a portion of my ownership share because I believe the continued success of the single would generate attention and bring me more production projects. In the end, I think I made the right decision.

Just His Luck

As I stated earlier, the business side of remixing can get tricky. One of my colleagues landed an opportunity to remix a song that was a number one hit single on the Billboards' Hot 100 chart. The track featured two of the most popular Hip-Hop/R&B artists in music today. My colleague created a club-style up-tempo track that contained hard-hitting drums, smooth strings and a vocal sample. The new remix had a unique sound and a different vibe from the original version. Excited about the new sound of the remix version, the two-featured artists recorded new lyrics and additional elements that took the remix to next level. The final result of the remix was arguably better than the original version.

Now, let's go over the issues at hand for the producer. The first issue was establishing his publishing share. Although the producer had done production work on several major releases, this was his first remix project. What he didn't know was that his remix would be considered a "derivative" of the original song thus entitling him to *zero shares of ownership*. Remember, as a copyright owner you are entitled to create a derivative of your own work. So, even though the producer created a "new track", the original copyright owners (including the producer of the original version) would all receive royalty income generated by the remix.

After getting over the disappointment of not receiving a publishing share and royalties, the producer attempted to negotiate a higher remix fee as a last resort. To his surprise, he was able to negotiate a fee that doubled his original quote. Right before the contract was signed, the record label put a halt on the deal because of a sampling issue. Ironically, the songwriters of the sampled recording were the same songwriters that created the original hit song and the new remix containing the sample at hand. What a coincidence! Taking advantage of a financial opportunity, the publishers who represented the songwriters charged the record label a $20,000 fee for the sample usage. Because of the sample fee, the record label decreased the producer's fee by $20,000, leaving him with half of what he originally quoted. It was just his luck.

Production Credit

It's all about getting people's attention and of course at the same time bringing them something of quality. -Cookin Soul

What is *"Production Credit?"* Well, according to the dictionary, a "credit" is an acknowledgment of something as due or properly attributable to a person. So, in the music world, a "Production Credit" is awarded to a person to acknowledge their music production on a piece of work. This seems like something that is easily obtainable for a producer right? Not so fast! "Credit" might be the single most important asset in the music industry other than music publishing. Just look at how some songs are promoted today. The new smash single "Produced by Joe Blow." The mention of the music producer can add a tremendous value to the success of the song as well as the future success of the producer. Even megastar Beyoncé is credited as a producer on the majority of her songs. Production credit is extremely important, not only to producers but also to anyone who can obtain it. Having credit when the song is highly marketed and promoted also provides the producer with free press and publicity. Professionally you can never get too much of that.

For today's music producer, "Credit" is more than just simple text in the liner notes in the packaging of an album cover but an acknowledgment or "props" within the music industry. Don't get it twisted either, shouting your name at the beginning of each beat doesn't exactly guarantee props by your peers especially since that's the cool thing to do ("Digga" On The Beat"!). Ideally, you want to be taken seriously and develop credibility within the industry. The only way to do that is by continuing to build a good reputation and receiving proper credit for quality production. This leads me to a few important points. The terms *"Ghost Production"* or *"Ghost Producer"* were essentially created as titles for an individual who does not receive credit. Why would anyone want that title? If I were a chef, why would I allow someone to take credit for a wonderful dinner I prepared?

I know what you might be saying, *but this might be my shot to get into the industry.* I slightly disagree with that statement. If you have the opportunity to become an intern or an apprentice at a production company, make sure you gain knowledge about the production business process. There is so much more to music production than programming beats and melodies. Don't assume that you will miraculously inherit your production credit by sharing your ideas with people within the industry. Like I said, a production credit is an asset worth a lot of money especially on a major label release. If a record is a success and you receive the proper credit, you will forever be linked to that success. If someone wants to recreate that sound or are looking for that quality work you will likely gain more business just because you were given the proper credit. Do you think people will care if you or I say, "I'm the one that really produced that song" when its not properly credited? The answer is NO, definitely not!

Bangladesh versus Cha-Lo

A few years ago, there was a public dispute between two producers over the Lil Wayne song "A Milli." Shondre "Bangladesh" Crawford and the songs co-producer Cha-Lo were feuding over who created the track. "Bangladesh" has gone on record and said that Cha-Lo's production contribution was minor and that he gave Cha-Lo an opportunity. While some of the details are sketchy, we know that Cha-Lo did receive a publishing share and "production credit" on a triple platinum album. I don't know any of these guys personally, but I do wonder why "Bangladesh" would be so generous to Cha-Lo if his contribution were so minor or limited? The major point that you should take from this situation is, no matter what anyone says that Cha-Lo did or did not do, he received a publishing share and production credit. That fact alone means he was instrumental in the creation of a hit record.

Finally, don't take your production credit for granted. Don't allow your music to be displayed without getting the proper credit, especially now in the digital era. Music is flying across the web in extreme amounts, try to tag your mp3 files and ask website owners and bloggers to add a production credit when publishing your work. No matter what stage of your production career you may be in, make sure you get the credit you deserve.

The Mixtape Is the New Album

Outside of the artist giving you credit in interviews or using audio tagging to attach your name to your music production, your production credit is typically given in a printed format. Production credits on mixtapes are no exception. Initially the mix tape was just a combination of a deejay's favorite previously released songs. Deejays would pick songs that they like and make a compilation album. The evolution of the mixtape has expanded and turned into deejays getting exclusive unreleased songs. Then it expanded again to almost 100 percent of the content being all new songs recorded to original production work. With these changes, the doors have opened allowing the producer an opportunity to promote, market or feature their work. Producer and deejay Don Cannon is well known for hosting mixtapes for established Hip-Hop artist. Cannon got his start as a producer by supplying this high profile artist with his original production works. The popularity of these original mixtapes help producers feature their work and they can start accumulating production credits to develop a professional discography. This can only happen if you know the importance of obtaining credit on all of your production work, including mixtapes. Make sure that you obtain all the credit that you possibly can by including your name on the mixtape artwork and your name encoded into the digital music file.

If you know your beat is going on a mixtape, demand credit. They aren't paying you monetarily so demand production credit. You can start establishing your career by placements on mixtapes so don't be discouraged about the money. If the music is successful, you can create a positive buzz that could lead to future work you will be paid for. Also, if the music you produce gains radio airplay, you can earn royalties. If the artist decides to put the mixtape out with the marketing support of it's record label, you may be able to secure future work by having your name publicized with the release of the mixtape.

Size and Location Matter

Don't think for a second that your "production credit" is 100% safe. Just because your name is printed or displayed on an album or mixtape cover, CD insert or embodied in a digital music file doesn't mean you'll be happy with the way it is presented. As we discussed earlier, "production credit" is as valuable to you as it is to others. The "others" can be managers, lawyers, artist, producers, sound engineers or anyone interested in receiving credit for production. Almost everyone in this game looks to add on to his or her credentials. If they're able to add a co-production credit to boost their musical resumes, they will attempt to make it happen, even if they didn't do the work to earn it.

In early 1997, I worked with a new artist signed to an independent Hip-Hop label. This was right before I signed a production deal with Un Rivera Productions. I had been doing a lot of production work with a few up and coming artists from my neighborhood. The word about my production skills had quickly spread throughout the community. One day I received a phone call from a guy identifying himself as a manager. We talked about the possibility of his artist and I working together. It seemed like a good opportunity for me, so I agreed to do 2 or 3 songs. After about a week, we began to work on several songs in the studio. During our studio sessions, the manager would stop in to see how things were going, make suggestions, give ideas, evaluate, etc. This was normal procedure and nothing out of the ordinary.

Before I knew it, I received call from the manager informing me about a production opportunity for a movie soundtrack. I couldn't believe this was happening so fast and I was very excited. The work that the artist and I created was finally about to pay off. To complete the deal, I needed legal representation. The manager put me in contact with a lawyer (which was a bad idea at the time), so I hired him to review and negotiate my production agreement. After reviewing the agreement, the lawyer said the agreement was "standard," "straight forward" and "fair." Well, I found out the hard way that his opinion was inaccurate.

A few months later, the record label released a music video and CD single for my song. I remember being so excited about my first production project being available in major record stores. I went to Tower Records to personally buy a copy and to finally see my name in the cover. What I saw hurt my feelings and taught me a big lesson. On the back of the cover was my credit *"Produced By Darrell "Digga" Branch For Six Figga Entertainment, Inc"* in a light colored small font right under the credit "CO-Produced By [The Manager]" in big bold print! I couldn't believe what my eyes were seeing. Embarrassed and disappointed are probably two ways to describe how I felt at the time. . .

Illustration 12.

In a situation like this, you can move on in two different ways:

1) You can get so upset that you're ready to physically assault somebody. This wouldn't be ideal because it's not professional and could lead to criminal charges.

2) You can double check and receive confirmation on all details pertinent to your credits. Nobody will protect your interest or look out for you in this industry like you will.

Over time, I learned how people attempt to build a career in music off the backs of others. The manager took the attention off of me by minimizing my production credit and highlighting his name and company. He did this by simply having the graphic designer use a smaller size text font on my displayed credit. In this situation, I did receive my credit but the visual appearance created the perception that my role was less important. In the music industry perception is key. If it appears that some one's name is larger or in a bolder font, it gives the perception that a particular person should be the focus of attention. This may not seem like a big deal until it happens to you. These are critical points in a provision of your production agreement. Don't overlook them!

Tagging

If you listen to my production work, you will probably hear the whisper of the words "Six Figga" at the introduction of the song. I started adding the "Six Figga" sample to provide a way for listeners to differentiate my production work from others. This is called a "tag" or a "drop." Today, tagging has become a common practice amongst producers and beat makers, as they are used frequently as a marketing tool. "Production credit is one of the most important things a producer needs for exposure. If people don't know you did the track, what is the point? That's why we include the C-C-C-C-Cookin' Soul tag on all our beats" says **Zock** from the Cookin' Soul production team.[xxvi]

However, I wouldn't suggest all producers' start adding tags to the beginning of every song. There is some debate about the overuse of tagging. Tagging can be viewed as a nuisance but if done strategically, it can be great promotional tool for the producer. There have been instances where executives and artists request for tags to be removed. The reasons:

1. *Too much self-promotion*
2. *Disturbs the vibe*
3. *Credit is already in the liner notes*

I look at tagging as being a "digital audio logo" for your business of production. It helps the consumer and listener identify your product (great music) with your business (your company). For example, do you know why people refer to a short-sleeve collared shirt as a "Polo

Shirt?" In 1920, Polo player Lewis Lacey decided to improve on a shirt design made famous by tennis player Rene Lacoste. At the time, Lacoste designed a comfortable short-sleeve shirt with a crocodile embroidered on the left side of the chest. Lacey decided to embroider a shirt with a polo player on the left side of the chest. In 1972, Ralph Lauren went on to create a Polo clothing line that included Lacey's famous design. The point is simple: tagging is a very common tool, but if you're creative, you can also use it effectively to promote your own brand. Be as original as possible when creating your digital audio tag to separate your work from that of the competition.

The Internet: The Copyright Killer!

The information highway also known as the "Internet" has revolutionized the way the world communicates. As a result, the Internet has also transformed the way the entertainment industry is able to market, promote, distribute and sell digital content. The Internet has made all forms of entertainment content accessible to any user who demands it. For example, video sharing websites like YouTube allow users to watch videos and stream music on demand. Major retail chains such as iTunes, Amazon and Walmart are able to distribute digital products like eBooks, videos and music on a large scale. Apple, the parent company of iTunes in particular, has even developed exclusive partnerships with major music labels to distribute their digital content throughout the world.

The Internet however has its major drawbacks. With accessibility also comes *piracy*. Users are able to access, share and redistribute unauthorized content. It's no secret that anyone with some basic computer skills and knowledge can illegally download digital content from the Internet. This has become a major problem for copyright owners as well as musicians, beat makers and producers. The Internet is like a tube of toothpaste. Once the toothpaste is squeeze out the tube, it's nearly impossible to put it back. This is what essentially happens when music becomes available in digital form on the Internet. Anyone can display, distribute, copy and perform your music with or without your consent. This is why I call the Internet the "Copyright Killer." The abilities and functionalities of the Internet have changed the way we have to protect copyrighted works. For beat makers and producers who are not on top of their copyrighted work, it may become a huge task to enforce copyright law to protect your work. Your beats can potentially fly all across the Internet if you're not careful.

For sample-based beat makers and producers, the Internet is an environment that could get you in big trouble. If you incorporate samples into your production without gaining the proper permission, you can put yourself in a situation where you may be sued for copyright infringement. As a business-to-business activity, sampling is a lucrative business for companies' controlling valuable publishing catalogues. If you sample all, or even a portion from another recording (copyright) and you distribute the new recording through the Internet, you can be sued. The new recording does NOT have to be for sale either. Distributing "borrowed" material for free is a common myth, especially when it pertains to "Mixtapes." Most beat makers believe that the mere fact that music is "free" or used for "promotional use only," that they are somehow protected against a copyright infringement lawsuits. Music publishers are very aggressive particularly when it comes to protecting the works of their writers. As a beat maker, you want a music publisher who not only collects money from the use of your songs but who is also capable of protecting your work by actively preventing the use of your songs without permission. From now and for years to come, the Internet will continue to be a copyright playground for the good and bad.

Leaked Music or Promotion?

Throughout the music industry, there has been an ongoing debate about leaked music and its effect on the artist and record company. "Leaked" music is the process of releasing finished or incomplete recordings to the public without consent from the owners, record company or artist. Sometimes an artist or record company intentionally "leaks" recordings. This is where the debate begins. Are there benefits when a beat maker's music is leaked? Or is this an excuse to test a beat maker's music without their consent?

Major labels create very detailed marketing and production plans that contain important dates and deadlines to complete recording projects. These plans also keep each department on task for completing the project by the set release date. For example, let's say Kanye West has begun work on his new album, his record label will set a future album release date anywhere from 5-12 months ahead of completion. This is to ensure that the employees, staff and creative team follow the proper marketing and production schedule. The time between the start and end of the project is where things may become chaotic for beat makers and producers.

As a beat maker and producer, the opportunity to be hired to do production work for a major label or artist can be a dream come true. The financial benefits for up-and-coming producers are a bonus but in some specific situations, producers take advantage of having the access to a "major placement" for personal gain. For example, let's assume that an unnamed producer is hired to produce a song for Kanye West's next album. After the song is recorded and all the studio work is complete, the unnamed producer decides to release the song (without the artist or record label's permission) to various media outlets including radio, blogs, websites and mixtape deejays in the effort to gain personal accreditation and exposure. The thinking behind the producer's strategy is self-motivated and simple. If people like the new Kanye West song, A&Rs and artists will likely recruit the producer to work on future projects. Depending on the producer's work experience, the mere fact that they produced a song for Kanye West may also be a huge marketing tool to attract collaborators.

Producers are becoming just as well known as recording artists. Some have a desire to self promote and unfortunately they don't mind doing this to the possible detriment of the artist. Some producers think that the song they have produced is so great that they *leak it* to radio deejays without respect to the artist. This is wrong for a few reasons. The artist and producer entered a partnership upon working together. The artist had faith in the producer to make a great product. That didn't include jumping the gun by releasing the music, thereby creating tension and distrust between you, the artist and the record label. In some cases, leaking music prematurely can destroy the record label's marketing and promotional plan. Producers should always maintain a high degree of professionalism and respect for the musical projects they are working on.

The Infamous Email

During my early years as a music producer, I probably created over a thousand beats. Unfortunately for me, it was a real challenge to save and archive my work. Digital audio software programs weren't readily available to consumers back then so most of my music had to be recorded onto analog 90-minute cassette tapes. Think about it: It would take about 55 cassette tapes to record 1000 beats about five minutes in length. If you ever used a cassette tape duplicator, then you know how hard it is to locate and duplicate music from one cassette tape to another. To put together what we referred to as a "Beat Tape" was a serious task. Today, we can store, catalog and search through hours of digital music located on a computer hard drive. With the click of a few buttons, we can play music files, organize a playlist and burn it on a CD. Back then I had to record my music onto a high bias Maxell cassette tape for artist and executives to review.

Eventually, I moved on to recordable CDs (compact disc), which was a huge upgrade as far as sound quality was concerned. The best part about using tangible sources like cassettes or CDs is the fact that I could keep record of the people I gave my music to. If I made 10 "Beat CDs," I knew exactly who had a copy or who could make a copy. Today, the "Beat CD" concept is obsolete. Most of us use the Internet to distribute and exchange music files either by using file storing websites or email providers such as Google. Of course with all forms of technology, there are a few drawbacks. An email containing confidential information can easily be delivered with the click of a mouse and end up in the wrong hands. Your beats can then be downloaded by a stranger and/or uploaded to the Internet with no possible way of knowing who is responsible. While it may be close to impossible to pull back a previously sent email, you can provide yourself some added protection in case your email with music attached ends up in the hands of an unsavory individual.

Copyright Email Disclaimer

An email disclaimer is a statement added to an outgoing email that gives notice to anyone not listed by you (the original sender). The statement explains in detail what an unauthorized individual should do if they have received your email in error. Adopt the following or one with similar language for your future usage:

"This email and any files transmitted with it are confidential and intended solely for the use of the individual or entity to whom they are addressed. If you have received this email in error or not from the original sender (Copyright Owner Name Here), please notify the (Copyright Owner Name Here). This message contains confidential information and is intended only for the individual named. If you are not the named addressee you should not disseminate, distribute, copy, download, alter or edit the files in this e-mail in anyway. Please notify the sender immediately by e-mail if you have received this e-mail by mistake and delete this e-mail from your system. If you are not the intended recipient you are notified that disclosing, copying, displaying, downloading, editing or distributing or taking any action in reliance on the contents of this information is strictly prohibited. Any infringement of copyright will be enforced."

Selling Beats Online

The Internet is probably the most useful form of communication in the world. It is also the biggest marketplace for digital products. Anything that can be transformed into digital form can be transmitted across the Internet. The Internet has totally restructured the way music is distributed in the process. Online stores like iTunes, Rhapsody and Amazon are digital retailers for most independent or major record distributors who offer completed songs. There are also digital retailers who distribute incomplete or unfinished music to aspiring artist or musicians looking to make it big in the game.

Over the last 5 years, there has been an emergence of websites that focus specifically on selling music created by beat makers and producers. Unlike music available at traditional online retailers, most of the music for sale on these "beat selling" sites is original instrumentals or unfinished compositions. Although there are hundreds of beat selling sites online, most of them use the same business structure. The game of selling beats online revolves around three major players:

Beat Maker/Producer

Beat makers or producers are the licensees of the copyrights. They supply the website with the music content and grant the website the right to display, distribute and sell their work to users and/or members on the website. Most sites allow beat makers and producers to set up profile pages to display their music, contact information, photos, etc.

Users/Members

Most beat selling websites are designed with social networking capabilities allowing people to become members. Members or users of the website are able to obtain rights to music created by the beat making members of the website.

The Website Entity

The website entity provides a service to all its members. It usually handles all technical, legal and financial matters between the beat makers (Sellers) and users (Buyers).

Legal Middleman

Once you get pass all the fancy graphics, flash effects and technical features on beat selling sites, the underlying theme surrounding all beat selling websites revolves around only one thing, the copyright! In order for these sites to operate and provide a service to its users, it needs to obtain several exclusive rights from copyright owners. These sites couldn't exist without beat makers providing the music.

Uploading Beats To A Website Server

You need to be aware of your rights when uploading your music onto a server. Remember copyright law (see "Copyright Ownership" on page 94) gives you the right to sell, display, perform, distribute and reproduce a copyrighted work. So in all actuality, the owners of the website (and in some case the owner of the server) need to be granted permission from you just to copy your music onto its server. Pay special attention to the following points when uploading beats:

Exclusive/Non-exclusive Rights

Once the website entity has obtained the right to upload your music, they will also need to be granted the rights to license your work to other users. Most sites will give you two options to transfer your rights:

> a. **Non-exclusive** - The website entity will give users the option to buy tracks under a non-exclusive agreement. This option allows the producer to retain all rights and issue licenses to multiple users.

> b. **Exclusive** - The website will give users the option to buy a track under an exclusive agreement. This option gives the user the exclusive right to a single track.

Displaying On A Website

The website owner will definitely need the right to reproduce, distribute, sell, promote and advertise your music on the site. They also will need the right to display your name and likeness too.

Production Credit

Make sure you require the website entity to provide clear and legible production credit in the metadata field of downloadable copies and on the website.

Watermarking

Watermarking is an audio "tag" or production credit that discourages someone from making unauthorized copies during streaming. Unlike a watermark on a visual image, watermarks are embedded into audio files of the original tracks. Most beat makers insert audio tags at the beginning of each track as a precaution anyway.

Derivative Works

All users who wish to modify or make changes to music on the website must have permission from the beat maker or copyright owner. Modifications include additional instruments, vocals, harmonies or any elements not accompanied in the original work. It is imperative that the website entity doesn't allow users to assign, transfer or sublicense your rights in a track to any other person or entity.

Distribution

You should pay very close attention to how the website handles the distribution of your music. As the beat maker and copyright owner, you will need to give the website entity the right to distribute your music to its users digitally or in a tangible form such a CD. Most beat selling sites deliver digital content to its users by email. Content delivery should be clearly specified in your agreement to ensure that your music is only being delivered to the user requesting the rights.

Synchronization of Music

Up to this point, we've been focusing on basic distribution rights and licensing but there is another right users may need. A synchronization license can be bought either separately, or along with a distribution license. This license gives users the right to synchronize the beat with images in a motion picture, television show, student film, short film, slide show, video game, or any other visual media as background music. Users may also want to use the beat for a scene, commercial, etc.

Copyright

You should always maintain ownership of your contribution to the new work. The worldwide copyright of the composition and master recording should remain 100% property of the producer.

Public Performance of the New Work

The user shall have the right to perform the new work publicly. Make sure the website entity requires the user to register the new work with a Performance Rights Organization such as ASCAP, BMI or SESAC and to afford you (the producer) no less than 50% writers credit when registering.

Keys to Selling Beats Online

Selling beats online can be a great alternative for beat makers looking to earn money, build a fan base and feature their talents. However, selling beats online can also be very competitive. Most popular beat selling sites have thousands of beat making members with over 10,000 beats for sale. It's not only difficult for beat buyers to find music to buy, its also difficult for the beat maker to sell them. Having name recognition helps. People scroll through the pages to search for producer names they recognize. The producers with a following usually sell more beats and receive greater exposure.

Even if you decide to sell beats on your own website, you will still be faced with the obstacle of attracting beat buyers. You have to build up your reputation within the market and direct people to go to your site.

Here are some useful strategies:

1. *When choosing a beat selling website, focus on the function-ability and e-commerce features*. You need a website that is easy for users to navigate and buy beats fast and easy. Don't get caught up in all the fancy graphics and entertainment value that some websites provide.

2. *Attract beat buyers to the website by promoting yourself every chance you get.* Educate potential buyers on the online beat buying process. Don't assume that buyers know what to expect when they arrive at the website. Use the website as your "storefront" to feature your work and conduct business accordingly.

3. ***Put together an affiliate marketing team.*** Find a few friends willing to promote you for an exchange of a percentage of sells they bring in. There are aspiring artist looking for music everywhere. Tell a friend to tell a friend!

4. ***Develop your own website to establish your own brand and identity.*** If you can afford to create and maintain your own website, this would be a great option. Having your own website separates you from the competition allowing you to increase your price for beats and build your own customer base. You will also have more control over the type of licensing arrangements you can offer potential buyers.

5. ***Take time to choose attractive names for your beats.*** Naming your beats is a critical decision that most beat makers take for granted. Choosing a bad name can be the difference between a beat maker attracting a buyer and getting a sale. A beat name is the first thing that gives the buyer an idea of what they expect to hear. Name your beats is an art that calls for you to be as creative as possible to market your music. As a buyer, which beat would you prefer to play: (1) "Track 1" or (2) "Jeezy Head Banger?" I would choose (2), because it sounds much more attractive and it makes me want to hear what a "Jeezy Head Banger" sounds like. "Track 1" is way too generic.

6. ***Categorize your beats by genre.*** If you create beats that fit into a certain musical style, group them together to make it easier for buyers to narrow down their selections. It is also important to help buyers from different geographical locations to identify the musical style they are most interested in. Although it may seem like a cliché to use terms like "West Coast," "Down South" or "East Coast," many buyers identify with these terms to classify a music styles.

7. ***Set an appropriate price for your beats.*** Setting a price can become a difficult task. Depending on how high or low you set your price will determine different results. I believe the best strategy when selling beats online is to concentrate on selling a high quantity of beats at an affordable price. Many beat makers waste time waiting for one or two buyers to pay them $100-200 dollars for one beat. The same beat maker could have sold 4-5 beats for $25 dollars in the same amount of time. Through my

limited research, I discovered that most websites sell non-exclusive beats for about $25. You want to stay competitive but you don't want to devalue your production work either. If the website attracts high paying buyers, use your judgment and be flexible with adjusting your price.

Mixtapes

A Mixtape is collection of songs usually compiled by a deejay and recorded onto a cassette tape. In the early years, there were two-forms of mixtapes. The first was a compilation of selected music with a specific theme or mood that reflected the musical taste of the deejay or host emcee. The second was more of a "party" mixtape that contained recordings from social events, club performances or parties. Deejays such as Grandmaster Flash, DJ Hollywood, Afrika Bambaataa and others would record club performances onto cassette tapes and sell copies for upwards of $75 per tape.

Today, technology has helped "the mixtape" evolve into a digital promotional tool. Deejays are not recording onto cassette tapes but are now creating MP3 playlists and CDs (compact disc) as ways to distribute mixes. And although, the cassette "tape" is no longer the choice medium for distribution, the term "mixtape" is still commonly used to refer to mixes on CD, MP3 or any other form of media.

Technology has also broadened the definition of "the mixtape." Before, a mixtape would be distributed locally in mom and pops stores or out of the trunk of a car. Today, mixtapes can be downloaded online by way of the Internet onto all kinds of devices like cell phones. Mixtapes are sometimes even packaged just like a major label release. So, technically almost any compilation of music that is not distributed through major retail music channels are considered to be a mixtape (even though at times mixtapes are also being sold through major retail stores such as Best Buy, iTunes or FYE).

So, your next question should be: *What is a mixtape again?* At this point, I'm also confused about the definition. The uses of "mixtapes" and their distribution change depending on the purpose of the mixtape and who creates and/or distributes them. I do know one thing though:

The term "mixtape" creates many legal issues for a producer.

Album Vs. Mixtape

To truly understand how a Mixtape creates legal issues, let's look at the difference between albums compared to Mixtapes:

Independent or Major Album Release	Mixtape
Retail Price of $17.99	Free
Production credit in liner notes	May receive production credit; only if artwork is available.
Creative control	No Control. Whatever the artist decides to release to the public stands.
Producer royalties	No royalties for sales of CDs or downloads. Nothing.
Advanced Fee Payment	In most cases, the artist or deejay will not pay for production on mixtapes.
Mechanical royalties	Songwriters don't get paid for mixtapes.
Production agreement with record label	No legally binding agreement between anyone.

Chart 1.

As you can see in the chart above, the mixtape does not provide the producer with the same legal arrangement that an album does. As a producer and copyright owner, you will discover that anyone who wants to display, perform, distribute or sell your music has to get permission from you; even for usage on a mixtape. The way music is freely used to create mixtapes is why the entire concept of the mixtape is a big legal time bomb waiting to explode. The fact that anyone can collect a group of songs and distribute them by way of the Internet or CD is illegal.

The topic of illegal downloads, Internet privacy and file sharing can fill up a book by itself; and the new concept of the mixtape only adds to the issue. Over the last 10 years, record stores have been raided, deejays have had their studios raided, and even consumers have been arrested in cases involving illegal downloading. While these are examples of isolated cases, they do prove that copyright laws can be enforced on a major scale.

For Promotional Use Only

Deejays have found a creative loophole to release Mixtapes by acknowledging that the mix is for "Promotional Use Only" and intended to promote the "music" for sale.

In the Hip-Hop industry, the mixtape has become a major promotional tool for recording artist signed to a major label. The idea is for the artist to create tracks for a mixtape in hopes of building momentum and anticipation for the "real" album that will be for sale. The mixtape is used as a big promotional vehicle, which is great for the artist and producer, but in most cases, the producer's rights are violated based on a lack of communication and proper protocol. For example, music producer the RZA and rapper The Game collaborated on a track for an upcoming album by The Game. The track was eventually rejected because administration issues involving the track weren't resolved before the album deadline. What happened next created the real issue. Without permission from RZA, the track was added to The Game's mixtape and distributed online.

Let's recap, the song was for The Game's upcoming album to be released *for sell*. Administrative issues like sample clearances, advanced payments and publishing splits were not resolved. This didn't prevent the song from being added to a mixtape promoted by The Game and distributed *for free.*

According to Game, RZA said he could have the track. "[RZA] came to the studio and brought the track to me. He's like, 'Yo Game, this is for you.' You can have that. Those are his words."[xxvii]

But was it RZA's intent for his music to be released for free online? Issuing a statement through his assistant, RZA said "this is business and in all fairness, it would have been cool if they would have just let us know what the intent was, because we began soliciting the track for purchase and it looks like this was a double sale issue when it wasn't." Communication of intent should be clear to parties involved from the beginning.

To prevent this mishap, a simple agreement could be drafted and signed by both parties. This should protect your music from being released on a mixtape if the clear intention was for the track to be used on an album release. If an artist intends to add your production to a mixtape, you should be notified and a presented with a production agreement. This will serve as protection for all parties involved.

Production Disputes

After spending so much time developing your craft, building relationships and sharing your music with the world, the last thing you want to do is fight over what is rightfully yours. Don't think that an iron clad contract agreement will keep you safe from having issues. Even having the best attorney in the world won't shield you from a production dispute. In some cases, production disputes arise because an agreement is not in place at the beginning. In Hip-Hop music, there are thousands of reasons why legal disputes develop. On the surface, most production disputes may appear to be complicated legal disagreements. In short, the majority of issues revolve around one factor: copyright law.

Selling Beats to Multiple Artists

This is a very common issue for beat makers and producers at all levels including the most successful producers. In most cases, this happens because the beat maker or producer has either:

1. Previously entered into an exclusive license agreement with another party.

2. Intentionally entered into multiple agreements with multiple parties to receive multiple advance payments.

Not Clearing Samples

Sample disputes are very common in Hip-Hop music. Many sampling issues occur because beat makers are uneducated about the legal aspects involved in sampling. There is a fraction of beat makers and producers who still believe that any sample, one measure or less in length is perfectly legal to use without consent from the copyright owner. Not needing permission is a huge myth that often causes beat makers and producers into misleading the artist and the recording label to believe that no samples are included in the master recording. Don't damage your integrity or professional reputation for dishonesty or negligent behavior.

Royalty Payments

Royalty payments are made based on the percentage of income derived from record sales. If a song becomes a hit and sells millions of copies or downloads, a beat maker or producer could earn huge royalties. After the advance, additional fees and reserves are deducted, royalty payments are supposed to be issued to you. Of course, that doesn't always happen. Over the last few years, various lawsuits have been filed against Hip-Hop artist Lil Wayne and his record label Cash Money Records over non-payments of royalties. Producer Jim Jonsin sued Lil Wayne for $500,000 over nonpayment of royalties for production work on one of Lil Wayne's biggest singles "lollipop."[xxviii]

Mixtapes

The entire premise behind the "mixtape" conflicts with every aspect of copyright law. A mixtape is nothing more than a concept name used for putting a collection of songs together and presenting it as one single body of work. You may be thinking, *isn't that what a full-length album is?* The answer is yes but unlike an album, a mixtape is free and contains music that hasn't been licensed legally from copyright owners. This causes major issues for beat makers and producers. Its not uncommon for an artist to release a mixtape containing beats with unauthorized samples. Although the song is featured on a free mixtape and not an actual retail album, current copyright laws state that unauthorized samples can only be used for educational use in a classroom or to comment upon, criticize, or parody the work being sampled. 50 Cent is a defendant in a lawsuit over an unauthorized sample on a mixtape at the time of this writing.[xxix] Robert Poindexter is suing 50 Cent over the unauthorized use of "Love Gonna Pack Up and Walk Away" on "Redrum," a song included on 50 Cent's War Angel Mixtape. The verdict in this case will set the precedent for how beat makers should handle sampling use on mixtapes.

Real Situation

There was an interesting dispute between Pittsburgh rapper Mac Miller and D.I.T.C. co-founder/producer Lord Finesse that caught my attention.[xxx] The heart of the dispute surrounds Mac Miller's use of the Finesse-produced instrumental "Hip 2 Da Game" on his K.I.D.S. mixtape released in 2010. In the suit, Finesse claims that Miller sampled the instrumental without permission. Unlike the 50 Cent case, Finesse is an established Hip-Hop producer who uses sampling techniques in his production. One might assume that Finesse would be agreeable and acceptable to another Hip-Hop artist using his music, but considering the current trend of using classic Hip-Hop tracks as a musical soundscape for free mixtapes, you can understand why Finesse wants to be compensated and credited.

While Mac Miller's success might not be directly tied to Finesse's song, the issue speaks to a larger point of how free mixtapes generate money for artist without compensating beat makers or producers who, in most cases are unwilling contributors. Artist such as Mac Miller are able to generate respectable income from show performances, endorsement deals, merchandising deals and other revenue sources. In most cases, the beat maker or producer can't share in any of these revenue streams.

Half Time

Congratulations to you for making it this far. We have gone over a lot about music production and many of the key components that directly affect the beat maker and producer. Part one was designed to put a special focus in the areas of music production, management, law, publishing and more. Part two is designed to help YOU recognize and develop your hidden talents through self-evaluation. The hope is for you to use part two as a guide to self-development and discovery. As a beat maker or producer, you will need the resources provided to design *winning strategies* to navigate throughout the industry. The music production industry can be a brutal place if you're not prepared for it.

To reach your goal of success, you need to be prepared with much more than just "hot tracks." Musical talent and technical skills make up only about ten percent of what is needed to become a well prepared and efficient beat maker or producer. Over the next few chapters, I will focus on areas of development to help beat makers and producers. Preparation, imaging, studio etiquette, artist development and networking are topics that will be covered.

Beat Maker versus Producer

The origins of the phrase "Beat maker" derived from the act of making Hip-Hop beats, which creates Hip-Hop music. There are people that are just beat makers and then there are people that are producers. So what's the difference between a beat maker and a producer? Well, to put it simply, anybody can make a beat. You can make a beat by hitting on a table. The difference between a producer and beat maker is... [pause and take a deep breath]...it's ENORMOUS. Let's look at Quincy Jones, James Brown or George Clinton as our examples. Half the time as music producers, they didn't have to touch an instrument. They would instruct musicians on how to play instruments in a way that would achieve the sound they were thinking of originally in their heads. That's what you call a producer! They hear a song in their heads before it's recorded— which includes the vocals and instruments. When you have free software production programs readily available, anybody can make a beat but that doesn't make you a producer.

Production is when you develop a complete concept for an entire music project. A producer can already hear how a vocalist should sound on a song before it is recorded. When they do record, a producer can coach that person through the whole track to achieve the desired sound. Beat makers put sounds together in a form of a "beat" or rhythm phrase and leave it at that. A producer knows pitch, range, where the drummer should break, where the guitarist should riff, when the singer should hum, laugh, hit their high notes and when to add a sample, etc. Producer Hi-Tek had an eye-opening experience when offered a production opportunity by super producer Dr. Dre. "It was like [if you want your production credit] 'come out and produce.' I was on a plane the next day. Now, I really understand what he means. You can't really call yourself a producer unless you're in the studio producing."[xxxi]

The title "beat maker" is more of a label that describes a job function or skill in which most Hip-Hop producers should possess. So, in theory, a producer can also be a "beat maker" but a beat maker can't be a producer without the possessing the necessary production skills and training.

Stick To Your Guns

Ralph Waldo Emerson once said, "Wise men put their trust in ideas and not in circumstances." Successful music producers build trust between the artist and themselves. They don't allow any circumstances or preconditions to affect their vision. Producers build trust within people by displaying confidence, integrity and creativity. Let's face it, anyone can come up with an idea but it's hard to convince people that the idea is great.

Producer and co-founder of Def Jam recordings, Rick Rubin is a prime example of a producer who gains trust amongst the artists he works with. Rubin has produced music for artists such as Jay-Z, Johnny Cash, Red Hot Chilli Peppers, The Dixie Chicks, U2 and more. He has produced music in different genres such as Hip-Hop, Country and Rock. In order for any person to accomplish that kind of success, they definitely need to be skilled *and trusted*! Outside of his great skills in sound and arrangement, Rubin also has the ability to get the best performance out an artist. When you build a relationship with an artist and more importantly, they trust your judgment, you will produce great results. It's a skill that leaders have to embody in order to be effective. Coaches, CEO's, movie directors, presidents, parents and music producers all have to pull the best out of their artists, clients, students and or children. It's all a part of the job. Being great is definitely expected of a leader. Production is deeply connected to trust. People have to trust the producer's judgment. To build trust, people have to believe that you will lead them with a clear vision and have a sense of integrity.

Values & Integrity

Next time you're working with an artist, you need to ask yourself this question: *How do people respond when I present a new idea?* If the usual response is "filled with skepticism" or "apprehension," people don't trust your judgment and may question your musical talent.

The one thing that separates "super" producers such as Dr. Dre, Timberland and Swizz Beatz from other producers is the *"trust factor."* They allow trust to be the motivating factor behind their artistic integrity. Artists that work with these producers believe that they will carry out their vision and deliver high quality work. The ability to build a high level of professional trust within people is the key and most important factor. You can be the most talented music producer in the 21st century but if artists don't believe in your work and have faith in you, talent becomes a mute point. As producers, we tend to focus on getting attention and exposing everyone to our creative talents. During the process, it is equally important to make people aware of why your production is valuable. A good producer creates value by being trustworthy and making correct decisions musically. So, when an artist doesn't agree with a producer's decision musically, an artist will trust the producer's artistic direction.

Your "net worth" is not your actual worth in dollars but it is your potential to make a dollar. Your value is the faith and belief that people have in your work. You work hard to produce a good product and people respect you for that. People expect a high quality of work from you. That is all a part of building a valuable brand.

Your skills, talents and other musical capabilities measure the value in your earning potential. Sharpening your assets and developing your skills only further increase your value. Don't sell yourself short by lowering your standards. Always keep in mind that as a beat maker, you will be judged on your skills. As a producer, you will be judged on your values and abilities to oversee a project.

Persistence

The golden opportunity that you seek lies within yourself. I only know of one road to success and that's the trail marked by persistence. When I was working on Cam' Ron's debut album "Confessions of Fire," we recorded at The Hit Factory studio in NYC for about 5 months.

During that time, I got a chance to meet many of today's popular artist and producers like The Trackmasters, Swizz Beatz and Busta Rhymes to name a few. Being the new kid on the scene, I was just happy being in that type of environment. Many producers use to come by the studio to play music. I specifically remember one guy who never got the chance to play his material. He would sit on the floor outside the control room while Cam' Ron would be recording inside. I don't believe he ever got a chance to submit music for Cam' Ron's album but the persistence to show up every few days made everyone realize how serious he took his craft. Three years later, that producer went on to produce one of Cam' Ron's biggest singles, "Oh Boy." The producer's name was Just Blaze.

Preparation
Are You Ready?

Have you ever heard the saying: "poor preparation equals a poor presentation?" That phrase is most definitely true. If you don't prepare for a meeting how successful could the meeting actually be? Who wants to go to a meeting that could be financially rewarding and wing it? As a producer you are going to have to sell yourself and your product, the beats. You must know who your going to see, who you're playing beats for, what are their musical interests, what direction they want for their specific projects and so on. Using professionalism rarely fails: always be professional. Go into every meeting with a clear goal in mind, understand the needs of your audience and be a good communicator.

As producers and beat makers, it is your job to make music that inspires artist to write and record to. Sometimes the vision behind your music needs to be communicated. The concepts have to be made clear. You have to communicate these thoughts and sometimes even use persuasion to get an artist to bite. Walking into a meeting knowledgeable about the artist and what they are trying to achieve is powerful and you gain much more respect that way. You are able to prepare and come with beats that won't waste everyone's time and energy. Most beat makers have hundreds and hundreds of beats that they are ready to sell. Most A&Rs and artists don't have time to sit around while you play everything off your hard drive. Do your research ahead of time and come prepared, ready to close the deal. Part of preparing is having your materials ready in advance.

High Quality Products

You should always have high quality beats on your drive. The beats should be mixed, arranged and complete. If you consider yourself to be a "business," your product should always be of the highest quality.

You must remember that your product directly reflects you and the opinion others will have of you and your work. Keeping that in mind, your product should always sound great, no exceptions, and no excuses. Why would you make a CD or MP3 file full of music that sounds incomplete or distorted? Why would you give someone a CD that looks old or warn out? Why would you send out an MP3 file with incorrect metadata? Your music is a representation of YOU! If you want respect and credibility, you need to practice high standards regarding quality. An opportunity may present itself and you might not be ready because your beat CD sounds horrible.

Quick Story

I went to a studio to play some tracks for a well-known artist. There were many producers waiting in line to play their tracks. Finally, after about 30 minutes, I went inside the console room and loaded my CD into the player. The tracks blasted through the speakers with hard energy and clear precision. Everyone in the room went crazy with excitement. I remember the well-known artist saying " your stuff sounds so clear and ready, it was dead in here before you played your beats." I attribute that to the time and effort I put into mixing and arranging my tracks. I prepared for that moment way in advance.

In order to create moments like the one I just described, you have to build a work environment suitable to create your music in. Try to design a comfortable studio but don't overdo it. Famed artist and producer, Dr.Dre said this about producer Hi-Tek: "Tek, you make your best music in your comfort zone, which is Cincinnati." Hi-Tek's response was "I think that's 90% true. I think a lot of my influence come from my surroundings. Me growing up in Cincinnati, it just gives me that original feel."

If you leave the lasting impression that you planned to leave, people will want to get in touch with you. Carry business cards with your phone number, email address and other contact information printed on them. If you're lucky, somebody will want to buy a beat or want you to come back to play beats in the future. Remember, making and maintaining contacts in this industry is essential.

Branding

When we think of an image, many times we think about a two-dimensional picture or photo, but an image can also be something that a person remembers. The image doesn't have to be real or a representation of reality. It can be an abstract thought or any figment of your imagination. For example, when a person walks into a job interview, the interviewer will have a perception of the interviewee based on the visual image first, while listening to what the person says in the interview second. If a person interviews for a job, and is spot on with their answers, but doesn't look professional, the interviewer's visual perception may stand in the way of the interviewee getting the job. The key word I just mentioned is "perception." Perception is the process we use to receive information with our mind. To really understand perception, you'll have to delve into the field of psychology, and that's a different book. For our purposes, perception is very important. When people have preconceived notions or image of someone, they tend to believe their views, whether the notion is accurate about a person or not. We also use our past to judge or make perceptions about people.

For example, you may have bought a product because of its reputation. Many of us buy designer clothing because we perceive it to be the higher echelon of clothing lines. Likewise, you may have made certain purchases of clothing because you want to affect others perception of you – that you're rich or well off, based on their experiences or knowledge of those clothes.

The Importance of Branding

When Jay Z was preparing to release his twelfth studio album, *Magna Carta Holy Grail* it was interesting watching the roll out. What caught my interest was how Jay Z featured music producers Rick Rubin, Timbaland, Pharrell and Swizz Beatz in the television and online advertisements. While viewing the ads, one would assume that these producers would collectively create a masterpiece based on their previous work with Jay Z. I believe Jay Z and his marketing team understood the value of bringing these musical forces and brands together to create the "wow" factor for the project. The most interesting part about the advertisement was, there were numerous producers who also worked on the project that weren't featured in the ads. These producers didn't have star power and weren't well known. Interestingly enough, Rick Rubin was featured in the ad, and he didn't work on the album at all. The marketing value that these four producers bring enhanced everyone's *perception* (there's that word again) about the album. It definitely influenced my opinion before I heard the album. You need your peers to value your work but you also want consumers to recognize and appreciate your talents as well. Value, perception and having integrity are extremely important. We will get into that later.

Image is Everything!

Why is this information important? Why does it matter how people perceive you personally and or professionally? There are several reasons but first you have to understand that image is everything. Don't think that because beat makers or producers are behind the scenes you don't have to worry about your image. Always keep yourself looking good, professional and presentable. In all honesty, you will be judged by how you dress. If you look like money, you will attract more money. If you look straight out the hood, right off the corner, no executive will consider working with him or her. Music production is a job with high and limitless earning potential, why miss out on potential earnings because you dress unprofessionally? Look like you want the job you are working for. Your skills won't matter if you don't look the part and create a lasting impression. You don't have to be "iced out", wear fake jewels, and "knock off clothing;" but your apparel should be neat and presentable. In addition, your body should be well groomed and clean.

Does it sound crazy that I'm writing that you should be clean and fresh? *Let's just say that because you smoke weed doesn't mean that everybody does.* Don't be fooled by the images you see on T.V. Try having your first meeting at Epic Records reeking from the "blunt" you had to calm your nerves. See how far that takes you or if you'll be invited back. If you want music production to be your career, you have to take it seriously.

Photo Imaging

A picture is worth a thousand words, and usually, even more. Photography and imagery are great tools to manipulate how the public perceives you. As I've mentioned, people tend to develop a view based on a preconceived images they already have in their minds. Photo images taken of you help form perceptions and further the image you want people to have of you. The great thing about photography is the control you have over what is perceived about you publicly. Of course, I'm not talking about the photos that the paparazzi may snap at you during an event or some type of unflattering moment. A professional photo shoot in a controlled environment is one of the main tools entertainers use to influence the perception of their image in the public. Think of all the images you've seen featuring artist like Eminem, Lil Wayne, Tyler The Creator and Drake. The images capture a moment that tell a story about the artist. Every specific detail inside a photo gives viewers information about how an artist wants to be portrayed. For example, if Eminem is sitting on the steps of a dilapidated trailer home, he is communicating a message to his audience through imaging. His message is intentionally left for his audience's interpretation. Guiding an audience's perception of you visually is what draws them in. Gaining visibility and a fan base that will buy your music is what effective branding can do for you.

Publicity

Publicity is the major component that fuels any marketing and promotion plan. Without the power of publicity, marketers and promoters can't control how the public perceives a product or individual. As we discussed previously, your name and image is important and it needs to be carefully developed so that the public will perceive you and your music positively. It is also important for you to be proactive in gaining exposure for yourself and your music. Is your music good enough to speak for itself? The answer is maybe and rarely. Is making great music enough? Not in most cases. Think of your favorite artist and the last album they released. I'm sure you heard audio drops on the radio; saw billboards, magazine interviews, blog articles, commercials on television and radio. The artist does all this whether they have a hot or cold single. If the well-known artist, who's out front and in public has to do this much promotion, it's safe to say you'll need to do a significant amount of promoting yourself. Remember, as a producer and business owner, you need to make sure people know your services are available. It's not enough to depend on your relationships with artist and executives or through "word of mouth" marketing. You need to develop a marketing and promotion campaign that encompasses as much publicity as possible. This requires hiring a publicist. A publicist is a person responsible for generating and managing publicity for you and your production company. A publicist does this work in many different creative ways. "As a publicist, I would incorporate my music producer client into the projects my other current clients are working on. There may be some synergy between the two" says publicist Lynn Hopson of Hobbiecom.[xxxii]

An effective publicist will get you attention, notoriety and exposure in unconventional places. If your publicist is gaining you placements that you can get on your own, then you need to reevaluate whether you are maximizing your investment. A publicist or PR firm should be able to open doors or other avenues of opportunities that you may not be able to do on your own.

Studio Etiquette

As a musician, artist or producer inspiration is the key ingredient to creating original music. There are other key components that are very important such as technical skill, personal interaction and most importantly the overall "vibe" of your creative session. Most industry professionals use a certain protocol or "*etiquette*" which are a set rules or guidelines to assure that the "feeling in the room" is positive and productive. In a normal work place environment like an office, there are general guidelines that workers are expected to follow. The studio environment should be respected in the same way. As a producer, you are expected to carry yourself as a professional. It is the producer's job to lead and set the tone for a creative environment. What exactly does that mean and entail? It's the producer's job to make sure everybody is focused and maintains a creative mindset. You don't want musicians in the studio more focused on the basketball game than the project at hand. You are creating a set of unwritten rules about conduct that make interactions between musicians, engineers and writers run smoothly.

Arrive Early

Make sure you arrive early at the studio. "Time is money" so if you can buy yourself some extra time by arriving to the studio early and preparing for your upcoming session; you will definitely benefit in the long run. Get comfortable with your surroundings so that you may run an effective session. Arriving to somebody else's studio early is similar to basketball players arriving early to an opposing team's arena to warm up. Players arrive early to get loose, comfortable, and familiar with the court. To have a good game, producers should feel the same way about a studio session. Not to mention the obvious:

You never want to make an artist wait on you. How would you feel walking into a studio and another producer is working with an artist you were supposed to work with because you were late? Better yet, a producer is playing his or her tracks and the artist starts to write lyrics to *their* beats. They are being creative with someone else and now you have to wait or reschedule. Worst-case scenario, they feel like they've found what they needed musically and you blew your opportunity. It can and will happen. *Bottom line - be prompt.*

Be Prepared and Organized

Preparation is the key to success. Do your research and find out as much information as possible about the studio environment that you will be working in. It's extremely important that everyone is comfortable during the creative process. Make sure that the studio is equipped with the equipment you need for the project including specific microphones, computer software and hardware. If it is necessary for you to bring your own resources, you should know what you would need in advance. For long distance, out of town travel or extensive work hours you need to make sure there are adequate resources for dining and lodging.

Dialogue

Remember, communication between you and all the creative people involved in the project is important. The sound engineers, musicians and songwriters in the room all need to work together. As the producer, it is your job to make sure everyone is communicating with each other and share your vision. It is critical that your conversation with everyone in the room remains positive while keeping them motivated and inspired. As the producer, people will be looking for you to lead and guide them towards completing the project. Your voice will have a lot of power. Make sure you use it.

Body Language

Your body language can send the wrong message if you're not careful. We often assume that spoken communication is the only way to get a point across but facial expressions, eye movements and body gestures can also speak volumes. If you don't like what an artist is doing to your track, find a way to tell them without physically expressing it. Your body language provides clues as to the attitude or state of mind you may be in. Negative body language can be a turnoff to the artist, which is something you definitely don't want. If you're nodding or slouched down on the couch while the artist is recording, your posture communicates to everyone that you are uninterested. Your level of enthusiasm could persuade or dissuade efforts from the artist. Your actions could ultimately "talk" the artist out of wanting to use your music and even worse, talk you out of a check.

Home Etiquette

Just because your production setup may be located in your home doesn't mean you don't have to follow studio etiquette. In reality, most beat makers will do most of their work out of their homes, either by converting a small area into a workspace or constructing a large area in a basement. Either way, as a beat maker, it is your responsibility to transform the traditional living environment into a creative working environment. When I began my career, I had a small table with a mixer on top, a keyboard and a few other devices in the corner of my bedroom. Back then, most of the production tools were bulky hardware modules. Today, technology has enabled beat makers to move towards a computer-based setup, which allows for better mobility and is more easily accessible. Computers have become mobile studios and because of this, we tend to forget how our surroundings affect our creativity.

If you can create a work environment free and clear of distractions, your music will prove to be better. If you're taking music seriously as a profession, you will appreciate being able to close a door and have your own private workspace. This will create a better professional environment while allowing your creativity to flow freely. Nobody should be making beats in the kitchen while mom is cooking dinner. This may be an interesting concept for the Food Network Channel, but you will never get work done as a Hip-Hop music producer that way. Starting out, most working conditions won't be ideal but try to dedicate some kind of private space to your craft. If you must share common spaces like a kitchen or living room and you can still produce good work, you are a better person for it. However, I don't suggest it.

The Right Vibe

Once you decide on the location of your working environment, make sure you design it to take on your own vibe. The *ambiance* of your work area can help you stay focused and concentrate specifically on music. You can create the mood by adding colored lights, inspirational paintings or pictures, candles, and different aromas by burning oils and/or incense. Now, before you think this is a waste of money, think about how much time you will be spending in your studio. You should do everything in your power to give yourself an added advantage to be productive. Do whatever it takes for you to be successful. If painting your room a specific color enhances your environment thus improving the experience for you and colleagues, make that investment. Your studio should be a comfortable place where you and others will feel free to be creative and expressive.

To review, follow this list to help you begin your studio sessions:

1. Arrive early
2. Be prepared and organized
3. Keep dialogue positive
4. Be aware of your body language
5. Have etiquette rules for any studio setup
6. Create a positive vibe and ambiance

Selling Yourself

The art of selling beats has less to do with the actual music and more to do with selling yourself! Now what do I mean by selling yourself? Many times, in this game, the key to success falls within the realm of selling yourself. Selling yourself is not limited to any of the following, but it includes: singing your own praises, explaining your creative ideas, presenting your work and the effort behind it and expressing the energy and feeling behind your beat. In music, producers and/or beat makers spend a considerable amount of time selling themselves, their ideas and/or music works to artist or companies. Communicating your work to the best of your ability will mean the difference between getting signed, getting a check, or landing on an album. Nobody can sell your music and ideas better than you. You are the best and most capable for that critical job.

Selling yourself or your music includes a few tactics that involve persuasion, convincing, manipulation and aggressively pursuing your goal. Think about it in terms of real estate. If you were a real estate agent you would want to convince buyers that the homes they are looking at is their dream home and is being sold at a great price and it's *so perfect* that it probably will not be on the market tomorrow. Selling beats is not that different. You want the artist or label to believe in your work and your words. You want them to believe that your beat is *exactly* what they're looking for and that they are getting it at a great price. You have to leave them with the thought that some other company or artist might buy that very beat in your next meeting. If you master the art of selling yourself, it can carry you across many different careers. Having the ability to convince people that you have specific skills and are capable of completing task can also get you any job you desire. To be successful as a beat maker, you have to believe in your music before you can sell it to others. If you happen to be shy, inexperienced, or a quiet person, remember there is something inside you that allows you to create music that you hope people want to hear. Pull from within that creative spirit and build the ability to speak freely and proudly of your work, goals and success. To improve your confidence, you must have faith in your work and know your plan to have an impact on this game.

Code Switching

Have you ever changed the way you speak depending on who you are speaking to? Do you talk among your friends the same way as if you were on a job interview? The answer is no for most of us. The act of switching up your language is called "code switching." Code switching is a communication technique in which people alter their style to adapt with their surroundings allowing them to identify with different people.

Let's use the President of the United States as an example. Barack Obama can stand in front of a stadium of politicians and read his speeches using standard dialect and appropriate political jargon. The President stands upright and motions his hands only when necessary to emphasize his points with a clear and concise voice. The very next day he can go to the Apollo theater with a very different audience, and speak like a reverend, with the a pastor's rift and delivery, showing emotion with his hands, singing Al Green songs, and rarely looking at his speech. He knows his audience, and acts accordingly to spread his message.

As a beat maker or producer, you will be put in various situations where you may have to switch your communication style to get your message across. It is also very important that you know when code switching is an appropriate communication technique to implement. Here are some common scenarios in which code switching may be used:

1. *Social gatherings/informational Situations.* You will often find yourself in social situations where you will interact with people in an informal way. Most social gatherings are held at clubs, bars, listening parties, conferences, studio, sporting events, etc. Although these gatherings promote a more comfortable atmosphere, don't overlook the fact that you may need to change your approach even under these comfortable conditions, depending on who you may end up conversing with.

2. ***During negotiations.*** To get your point across in a meeting where decisions need to use language that you may not necessarily use on a daily basis. You need to know the appropriate vocabulary and statements for the point you are communicating. It's important to be very explicit when arriving at a decision. There is a big difference between telling someone "I'm satisfied with this agreement" and "I'm good."

3. ***Introductory meetings.*** When you are meeting someone for the first time, you may need to put your best foot forward by making a formal introduction. "Hello my name is Darrell Branch" is formal. "What's good? They call me Digga" is informal. Both introductory phrases may be appropriate depending on the specific social gathering you are in.

Your Music Speaks Volumes

You know the amount of time and effort you put into your music, you know when all the key elements and variables are present, you understand when a piece of music is sensational in contrast to something that's not even worthy of being an album cut. If you *keep it real* with yourself and make sure your work ethic is high, when you tell others, *Yo I got some heat,* they're going to believe you. Your word professionally will mean a lot to people. Your meetings will slow down if every week you're telling artists and A&Rs *I got that heat* but when they listen they are constantly disappointed. If they feel that you've made no changes or efforts to improve your style, it won't take long before they stop answering your calls. It will be extremely difficult to work with an artist if your music doesn't live up to the hype. The goal is to develop a good rapport based off of your work and honor. It's your reputation and responsibility that establishes an honest and trustworthy professional relationship.

Trademark Your Name

Using a name other than your legally given name (in some cases your legal name too) can cause you some legal problems in the future if you're not careful. Choosing a "professional" name is a critical decision that many beat makers and producers overlook, treating it as a minor thing. Of course, it's easy to choose a random cool name but the question is: will you be able to obtain a trademark to protect others from using the name? Your job is to sell beats and become professionally known. What good would it serve you to build up a name that you can't trademark or legally use? It is also extremely important to protect your name from others who might want to do you harm, those who may try to profit off of your name or style. Do you know why legendary Hip-Hop artist the Notorious B.I.G changed his name from Biggie Smalls? The answer is rather simple: *the failure to obtain a trademark.*

A trademark can be any word, name, symbol, or any combination that is used to identify a product. Essentially, it's a brand name that is registered with the U.S Patent & Trademark office. The U.S. Patent and Trademark office provides trademark owners with federal protection. Some benefits of registering a trademark include evidence of ownership, notice nationwide of the trademark owner's claim and jurisdiction provided in the federal court system. If you register your "professional" name, no one will be able to do business under your name, symbol or any combination that is used to identify you as the "beat maker" or "producer."

The process of acquiring a trademark can be as easy as doing a name search online and filing an application that cost $325. You can find more detail information at: http://www.uspto.gov/trademarks/index.jsp. The filing process can take a minimum of 6 to 12 months for a completion. If you decide to file a trademark yourself, be very careful and follow the directions provided by the trademark office.

Before you start the trademark registration process, you will need to do a thorough name or mark search. You can start by doing a basic search on the Internet to see if your name or mark choice is currently being used be someone else. The trademark office also has a database that enables you to do a name and mark search. I would suggest that you really spend as much time as possible doing your search to prevent your trademark application from being turned down. If you do find that your name or mark choice is being used, don't lose faith. It still may be possible to register your mark. One of the biggest myths about trademark law is that *registration* prevents others from using or trade marking the same mark or name. This is not entirely true. A federal registration of a mark is not mandatory but having one gives an owner several advantages along with putting a public claim of ownership on the mark.

The main purpose of trademark registration is to make the public aware that you are using a name or image to represent an individual or business. Unlike copyright law, a trademark doesn't give you universal ownership of the mark, name or image. A single registration of a mark only provides ownership of a mark or name under a particular class or category. For example, say you want to register the mark "Delta Music" for your production company name but Delta Airlines and Delta Faucets are already registered trademarks. Because Delta Airlines and Delta Faucets offer different products and services, trademark registration may be accepted from both entities based on the fact that they offer different products and services. It would be unlikely that a consumer would get Delta Airlines and Delta Music confused.

Once you have narrowed your name choice down to about two or three different names for your company, you will need to decide which class or category you would like to register your mark under. If you know how you intend to use the mark, the U.S. Patent & Trademark website has a goods and services list to help you identify your registration class. For example, Delta Airlines is a registered trademark under International Class 39 (the classification of Transportation services). If you intend to use the "Delta Music" mark to represent your production company, you can register your mark under International Class 41 (the classification of entertainment services). Even though both marks are similar because of the use of the word "Delta," the goods and services provided by each company are different. Avoiding confusion and a delay in your trademark is why registering you trademark under the correct international class is very important. Registering your trademark under the correct international class is very important. Doing this properly will avoid confusion and prevent delays in registration.

Let's say you are the owner of the "Delta Music" mark under the International Class 41. You decide that you want to print T-shirts with your "Delta Music" mark/logo on the front and sell them on your company's website. After doing some research, you find out that someone else is also selling T-shirts with a logo that resembles your own. *What can you do?* Can you stop them from selling the T-shirts? Can you sue? The quick answer is no. Remember, a single trademark registration only grants an individual or business ownership in a mark under a single International class. So, even if your trademark is registered in a single international class, that doesn't necessarily give you trademark protection in another class. *To sell T-shirts or any type of apparel, you will need to apply for trademark registration under International Class 002 (classification of Apparel).*

I would suggest that you consult with an entertainment or intellectual property attorney before deciding to file your trademark application yourself. A good attorney will be familiar with the documents and may have additional resources to do a more in-depth name search. There are also trademark servicing companies that can do mark searches to look up registrations, both state and federal. As a starting point, try looking up your name in a search engine such as Google or Yahoo. See what results come up. You may be surprised by what you find.

Why You Should Trademark Your Name

Why should I go through the trouble of trade marking my name? The answer is simple: You need to protect your brand. When you start making beats and becoming known, you are creating a brand. Music production is a very competitive marketplace and if you want to stand out and "brand yourself," you need to make sure that no one other than you can exploit your name. You don't want to spend so much time promoting your music and your name just to have someone else come along and pretend to be you. A registered trademark prevents anyone from using your mark without your consent. Here are the three reasons why you should trademark your name:

1. *Give notice.* The "TM" symbol constitutes a notice nationwide of

the trademark owner's claim. It lets the public know that you are doing business under the mark.

2. ***Evidence.*** A registered trademark is evidence of your ownership in the mark. If you ever need to protect your mark in court, your rights can be enforced even in federal court.

3. ***Foreign registration.*** A trademark registration only protects your mark in the U.S. but the registration can be used as a basis for obtaining registration in foreign countries. Your mark can also be registered with the U.S. Customs Service to prevent importation of foreign goods infringing on your mark.

Trademark Disputes

I had to learn about the importance of registering a trademark the hard way. After promoting my production company brand, Six Figga Entertainment, Inc. for over 10 years, I decided to finally apply for a U.S. certified trademark. Being young, naïve and ignorant about the trademark process, I didn't think I would have any issues with registration. After all, who would possibly use the same name "Six Figga Entertainment" right? Well, to my surprise, an individual was actually in the process of applying for the trademark during the same time. Nervous and concerned about what to do next, I contacted a trademark attorney for some help. What I quickly learned from him was that to obtain a registration of a trademark, the individual or business doesn't necessarily have to be the first to apply for registration. Trademark law provides certain protections against an individual attempting to register a mark that is in use by someone else. For example, let's assume that Apple, Inc., one of the largest and well-known companies in the world didn't register the mark with the U.S patent & trademark office. If I attempt to register the "Apple" mark, the Apple Corporation would have ability to oppose my application by providing proof of origin. In my specific situation, the other applicant applied for registration nearly 32 days before I submitted my application. Although, his application was filed earlier, I had the advantage as long as I could provide the appropriate evidence.

My first plan of action to obtaining my trademark was in the initial filing of my application. Because I have been actively using the trademark since 1997, I was able to file my trademark application under "Used In Commerce" status. That provided the U.S. trademark office with notification that my mark had been in use before the actual application date. The other applicant filed for a registration with the "Intent To Use" the mark in commerce. My attorney immediately suggested that I collect as many physical specimens that would show proof that I was using the mark before 2004. I collected everything from business cards, flyers, domain name registration receipts and most importantly, CD inserts. One CD insert in particular provided the sufficient proof I needed to support my claim. Cam'Ron's 1998 album release, *Confessions Of Fire* demonstrated my mark appearing over 9 times in the liner notes.

Needless to say, the examining attorney at the U.S. patent and trademark office agreed with me and allowed my trademark application to continue going through the registration process. The earlier-filed applicant attempted to make things difficult by filing additional motions to deny my registration, but to no avail. This experience taught me a huge lesson about brand equity. I spent almost 10 years of my career promoting, exploiting and marketing my brand to consumers without having a U.S. registered trademark. Without a registered trademark, it will be difficult to protect your mark against unauthorized users specifically in the event of a legal dispute.

Marketing Yourself for Placements

Marketing yourself to gain a placement on a music project is a lot like advertising yourself as a product. Imagine yourself as a candy bar. There are many types of candy bars available at the store. How will your packaging distinguish you from other candy or stand out amongst the competition? As a beat maker or producer, you need to ask yourself the same question. There are thousands of beat makers salivating at the chance to get their big break, so how will you stand out amongst the competition? Most beat makers and producers miss out on opportunities because they don't connect with the buying audience. If people don't know you or can't hear your music, you can't expect to be hired to work on music projects any time soon. An aspiring NBA player must showcase his or her skills on a high school or college platform before being recruited to play in the NBA. You must also have a platform to showcase your musical skills as well. What is your name? Where can I hear your beats? What makes your beats so special? How is your sound different from others? If you have a problem answering any of these questions, you need to develop a personal marketing plan.

A marketing plan includes strategies that detail how you intend to communicate with your audience.

A standard marketing plan revolves around a few key principles:

1. Who is your target audience?
2. What are the current trends?
3. What benefits can you offer?
4. What is your approach?

You need to be able to answer these questions in detail. If you have difficulty coming up with significant answers, you need to take a step back and deal with each accordingly.

Who is Your Target Audience?

Your target audience is divided into two groups: The industry insiders and the general public. The industry insiders are artist, writers, musicians, DJs, record and publishing company executives. The general public is music consumers, magazine reporters, tastemakers and even your friends and family.

What Are the Current Trends in Today's Market?

Most beat makers and producers use the Internet as the main platform for marketing. The Internet gives us a wide variety of options to be creative and connect with an audience. Social networking sites have become the main vehicle for beat makers and producers. "Our marketing and promotion is one hundred percent on the Internet. Grinding everyday on our website and Facebook, Twitter, Myspace and all. We handle all of it ourselves," says Bock from Cookin' Soul. YouTube, Instagram and Vimeo allow beat makers and producers to connect with its audience through video. Boonie Mayfield recognized that YouTube could create a following that not only admires your music, but also you as a person. "Once the videos really started getting a lot of attention, I'd be in other states where I've never been before, and people would recognize me. Many established producers whom I've looked up to even know who I am and show love."

I have also used YouTube to provide a resource for users looking for video tutorials in the areas of business and production. The response was so overwhelming that it inspired me to develop a video-sharing site called Online Beat Tutor. Taking advantage of the trends in the market help you gain visibility and establish a following.

What Benefits Can You Offer?

Are you bringing anything new to the game? If you have something unique to share such as a new style or skill, you may be able to use it as a marketing tool to increase the value of your brand. Producer and Drum Percussionist Arab Muzik is a prime example of an individual who has used his performing skills to leverage a niche in the market. By playing around on the MPC, he developed his drum performing skills by accident. He started to look at the MPC as a real instrument and became a master at it.[xxxiii]

What is Your Approach?

Will you aggressively market and promote your brand every chance you get or will you be selective and choose specific opportunities? The wrong approach can kill your chances at a major opportunity and damage your reputation beyond repair. One of the most common and annoying forms of marketing is promotional emailing. Sending unsolicited emails to random addresses looks unprofessional and sends the wrong message. You don't want to end up on email spam lists. Take the time to write an introductory email to each individual you may be able to build a relationship and partnership with.

Online Production and Marketing

Another way a beat maker or producer can market and promote is by becoming a member of an online production networking and marketing site. These sites provide various services to beat makers who are looking to sell beats online or submit beats for use on upcoming projects. PMPworldwide.com is a production marketplace for beat makers, producers, label representatives, artists and songwriters. Aspiring producers can join a community of artists, songwriters or label executives who are looking to buy beats for independent and major label releases. The site also boasts a network of over 13,000 registered buyers. Blazetrak.com is another networking site that offers users the opportunity to submit audio clips, video clips, images, or documents to industry professionals for review. If you decide to make production-networking sites a part of your marketing plan, I must warn you about a common misconception:

None of these sites can guarantee that your music will ever be heard. Although these sites may act as a "middleman" between you and the rest of the "beat buying market," you must understand that these sites provide more of an "opportunity" rather than a "service." If a site allows 10,000 of its members to submit tracks for use on a major project, how many tracks do you think are reviewed? Is an A&R going to listen to 10,000 tracks? I seriously doubt it. This is why submitting tracks on these sites are more like playing the lottery with aspirations of winning a jackpot. The probability of landing a placement may be much greater, but as the saying goes: "you gotta be in it to win it."

From a manager's standpoint, you must use many different sources. Production manager Sarah J recommends: :[xxxiv]

1. Utilize different blogs and websites.
2. Produce music for mixtapes.
3. Create a campaign for your production brand.
4. Develop a website to showcase your work.
5. Register with Production Network Sites such as iStandardProducers.com and PMPworldwide.com.
6. Travel to different cities.
7. Staying on A&Rs/Artists radar is key!

Finally, whatever marketing strategy you decide to go with, make sure your plan is realistic. If your idea of marketing is submitting your music to a few email addresses, make sure you understand the odds and probability of landing a placement. Even submitting beats on a music production market site won't yield high results without an effective plan to stand out amongst your competitors. Marketing yourself will be an ongoing process that will enhance your brand and bring attention to your production but it will not automatically lead to a placement. Don't get caught up in thinking a beat placement will enable you to stop marketing yourself for other music related revenue. In basketball, coaches focus on designing strategies to not only win games but also to *win championships*. An effective marketing strategy expands opportunities and builds quality relationships. "I try to use every opportunity to promote myself using my own website, visiting other producer networks, doing blog interviews and competing in producer competitions like Red Bull Big Tune," says Boonie Mayfield.[xxxv]

Quick Marketing Tips

1. Make good music.
2. Partner with an artist.
3. Build quality relationships with your peers.
4. Build relationships with bloggers, tastemakers, print & online press.
5. Build relationships with radio Deejays, Mixtape Deejays and online music distributors.

I Like Your Style

When I started my professional production career in 1997, I didn't know how to pitch my music to artists and record labels. I didn't know how to format a playlist or even if I should deliver my music on cassette, D.A.T. or CD. Eventually, I picked up the proper pitching etiquette from my producer colleagues such as the Trackmasters, Ski Beatz, Buckwild and EZ -Elpee. I quickly learned that there is an art to putting a "Beat CD" together. Before, I would put about ten of what I considered to be my best tracks on a cassette tape, make duplicate copies and distribute them to different artists or A&Rs who were looking for tracks. That was my basic strategy, but I learned quickly that pitching my music this way was more like playing the lottery.

Organizing Music

The first thing I had to do was learn how to organize my music by style or genre. At that point, I took for granted how incorporating sounds from different genres influenced the style of my production. Grouping beats by style and sample made it a bit easier to sort my tracks. For example, if I created a track that contained a sample with big sounding drums and a heavy guitar riff, the track would be categorized as a "Rock-N-Roll" influenced track. Categorizing and labeling tracks make it easier to group music based on style. Grouping also allows you to easily select music for artists and A&Rs who request a specific style of production.

Ordinary versus Mainstream

The second thing I had to learn was the differences between creating ordinary tracks and tracks with mainstream potential. Having my music accessible by category and style was only half the battle. I wanted to make hit songs that would gain radio airplay on popular stations. To do that, I needed to study the *commercialism* of music and its effect on radio. Commercialism is an attitude or ideology that puts market share and sales above everything else. I used the word "commercialism" because it describes the attitude I needed to create music that would be enjoyed by the masses. I also discovered that I would have to sacrifice a bit of my creativity to conform to current styles of music. That became a difficult task because I wanted my music to demonstrate my originality while still maintaining a level of commercialization. Let's assume that the top ten songs on an urban radio station's playlist share similar musical elements such as hard-hitting drums and simplistic melodies. My tracks with mainstream potential would also need to incorporate some sort of elements that emulated the current trends. Not at all am I suggesting that you imitate other production styles. However, there are huge benefits to creating tracks that have the same *commercial appeal* for listeners. Even using the example above, your job as a beat maker or producer is to come up with various ways that create hard-hitting drums and simplistic melodies without sacrificing originality.

Themes

The last thing I figured out while categorizing my music was the recurring theme throughout specific tracks. I determined that I could put together a selection of tracks that fit these themes. For example, the party track, the pop track, the up-tempo "Pussy Cat Dolls-ish" track, (insert your favorite pop group here), the street hit or club banger track are all themes that can help with pitching your tracks to specific artist or record labels.

It really doesn't matter what you've done in the past. You can be some no name, and make it as long you have the right music; which is great for upcoming producers. But producers have to stay on top of their games to continue to get placements. There will always be someone else coming with new joints and a new sound; then you won't be around next year.

So what is the point? Focus your attention less on working with 8 gazillion different artists and touting that inflated discography like it means something. It does, but not as much as bringing your unique sound to the game and creating your own lane. Right now people want to hear music again, they don't care about the names. Most of the beat makers behind the current crop of one hit wonders have never sold a track before, but they have a hit with an artist probably from the same hometown. Most likely coming from a region nobody has cared about since the Dust Bowl. What they do with their career from that point is all up to them. The challenge is to do it again, make it work and make it last.

Versatility

It is important in music to be versatile. Versatility as a producer will come in handy. Learning different styles and techniques will only further your understanding about the art of production. While being versatile you want to focus on what you do best and you don't want to get caught up doing too much. By doing too much I mean trying to do every style and experiment with every sound. It's important to master your craft by finding your own niche and comfort zone. If you stretch yourself to thin, you can never perfect one style or technique. Another down side to stretching yourself to thin is confusing the consumer. How can a manager or artist refer you to potential clients if they can't describe your style? If they're going through your music trying to see if you are a good fit for a project and you're all over the place with Pop, West Coast, East Coast, Down South and a little bit of Country, you'll definitely get skipped over. Nobody will think of you when someone asks for a Down South beat, they'll just go to a Down South producer.

I don't want you to think you can't show versatility because that's not true. If you're from the East coast and somebody asks you to make a down south beat, of course you want to be able to produce that. You never want to be limited but you just don't want to be all over the place. The most important thing in beat making is developing yourself and your own distinct sound. If you don't have your own unique sound, you will never stand out. You will be like every other producer trying to make it. Take the time to perfect your craft, which will distinguish that you are as a producer. In the long run, this will prove more sustaining.

There Is Only One You (Musical Trends)

There are so many things for up and coming producers to consider when determining how they plan to brand, market and sell themselves. As long as you guide yourself with the love of music a producer should be fairly safe. Music is trendy. What's here today is literally gone tomorrow. Music changes sort of like fashion. We wouldn't dare wear last year's fashions and neither would a producer make last years beats. The producer wouldn't make last years beats because they wouldn't be in demand and no one would buy them. That's why it is important to create original music with fine production qualities. You should always start with a production concept. This will guide you through the actual album making process. What should you consider while developing a musical concept? You should think about what you want to convey.

If you're doing a soundtrack for a movie, you should consider the movie, what is it about and how you want the viewer to feel while listening and watching? You should consider the artist. Who are you working for? What do they like, what is their style and image? You can't make music for Miley Cyrus and just think that a twist here and there will make it suitable for a Nicki Minaj. You have to take the artist, their style and performance into account when creating a musical concept. Some artists already have an identity and you have to produce within that. When they reach out to you, they are established: you have to bring your skills to enhance their established sound. Over the last few years in Hip-Hop, there have been a few trends that have dominated. Those trends include singing rappers with melodic monotonous cadences and down south influenced rap and cliché' slang terms transformed into choruses. Producers have to understand the market at the current time, be able to sustain it while also creating music that will elevate the game to a different or in some cases, higher standard. Nobody said producing was easy. It takes a lot of thought, hard work and originality.

Originality

There can be an argument made that there is no such thing as originality. Franklin P. Jones once said, "Originality is the art of concealing your source." Most artists and producers recycle old ideas or use older content in new ways. The key to being original has more to do with developing an authentic expression rather than simply creating something "new." Being authentic means expressing what you think and feel through your music. This is why it is important to develop and maintain your own style. Creating a beat doesn't necessarily mean your developing a style. Having your own style sets your work apart from everyone else's. Not putting thought and effort into your originality is the wrong approach to authenticate your music. Dare to be different with your musical creativity. Don't be afraid to use new sounds, new song arrangements and unique dynamics. This is how you can set yourself apart and be amongst elite beat makers and producers.

If five producers are doing the same style, what true value will you really have in today's game? It's not uncommon to hear beat makers mimic each other to get ahead. Technology has made it more accessible for beat makers and producers to use the same production tools and share sounds. FL Studio, a software program developed by Image-Line features a graphical user interface based on a pattern-based sequencer. This feature has made it much easier for users to program instruments using visual patterns and step-by-step editing rather than a physical performance. It's as easy as choosing an instrument, arranging squares into a pattern and pressing play. If you combine pattern-based sequencing with a universal sound set, you are bound to have users creating music with similar characteristics.

Originality helps you create your own lane and possible revenue. When your original style is sought after that's when you start calling the shots and stating your own terms. Being original has nothing to do with creating something new but rather perfecting what is already in existence. The challenge will be to take your ideas that people may think are terrible, and showcase them anyway. Your persistence will determine whether people buy into your "original" idea or style. The goal of every beat maker or producer is to not only strive to create a new style but to change the game.

The Haters (Naysayers)
TIME-OUT

"Why you wanna playa hate on me?" Sing that line from Chucki Booker's 1992 hit song every time you feel hated on (Google search "Chucki Booker"). There will be at least 10 people who will try to discourage you and stop you from following your dreams. Haters will never go away so be prepared to deal with it. These people can be business partners, close friends and even family members. The majority of people are scared to fail. That's probably the biggest fear in the world. When you succeed, it makes people feel uncomfortable. I look at it as a part of human nature. If people don't discourage you during your path to success, you're probably not moving in the right direction. "The crab in the barrel theory" will always be prevalent during your path. If you really want to be successful and follow your dreams, keep your ideas and hopes to yourself. Family and close friends are usually the first people to discourage you despite their love, admiration or respect for you. Family and friends are critical and sometimes merciless. They may not mean to be harmful but they can be disparaging and hurtful. In short, be prepared to be by yourself, not physically but mentally. Others will not always share your same goals and dreams that you set out to accomplish for yourself. If you're serious about your career, get focused and rid yourself of all negative influences to your path to success.

Going "Against the Grain"

We hear people say it all the time "you need to surround yourself with your friends and family." To a certain extent that's very true. Family and friends are good resources and support but there is always an exception to the rule. Although they are important players on your Dream Team, friends and family tend to have different goals, different habits or an overall different mindset than we do. They might like to drink and smoke while you don't. They might sleep late while you're an early morning person. I'm not saying there is anything wrong with people having different habits but think about how it will affect you. Some of us have friends and family that *just don't and won't get it.* They don't have the motivation to accomplish their goals so they don't care to help you or support you in accomplishing yours. It's way easier for some people to hate than support. *What should you do?* Develop thick skin and a closed mouth. Don't tell people your every move, what you're trying to do or who you are planning to work with. Some things should be proven by your actions with limited conversation. You heard the saying "show and prove?" That should be your attitude at all times.

Artist Development and Relationships

I've been fortunate enough to work with many artists who I admire and respect. This doesn't mean I necessarily enjoyed my experience while working with them though. You might be thinking to yourself "I would love to work with Jennifer Lopez or Beyoncé." But think about it, would they say the same thing about you, the producer? What if you're hired to produce music for a mega star that's not receptive to your opinion or evaluation? After all, they are professional artists and performers who are experienced in the production process. This example also rings true when working with unsigned artist as well. Unsigned artist are hungry but inexperienced. When they get to the point of signing a deal, they feel accomplished, sometimes like there's no room for improvement. They're at a point where someone is finally appreciating them for their talent. In their view, they've arrived and their style has gotten them this far, why switch up now? Experienced artists are resistant to change because they already have a system in place that works. New artists are resistant to change because they have a system that has led to newfound success. You should respect their views but always do your best to get them to see your vision.

Record companies hire established beat makers and producers that they have worked with in the past for one reason and one reason only: results. They know producers histories, abilities and are banking on them to bring out the best in their new artist. If an artist isn't receptive, how can positive results be achieved? For the established artist, things can be a little more difficult. The artist may be at a point where they trust only their own judgment or that of their inner circle. The problem with trusting your friends or inner circle is that they are often biased. By nature, they want to like what you're doing and this might not be the same taste of the average consumer. The established artist may also choose to exclude you from the recording process. Artists may opt to work with their normal associates instead of you, the beat maker or producer responsible for the track he or she is recording to.

Some producers may not care, but if you love music and are truly there to do the job of a producer, this could be insulting. Producers speak with their beats, they express emotions with their drums, and each high hat, snare and kick is an emotion reaching out to grab the listener. People who put their hearts into their creations should be an asset to the recording artist. The artist and the producer should share a passion and therefore be able to make a wonderful composition. After all, it's your work that's inspiring the song. Even if you're able to make music separately, nothing can ever truly replace the bond, the creative expressions, and the instant dynamics of recording together in a studio.

Producers speak with their beats, they express emotions with their drums, and each high hat, snare and kick is an emotion reaching out to grab the listener. Everyone has his or her own opinions and personalities. So as a producer, you have to be someone who is capable of understanding, flexibility and reorganization. While listening to your tracks in a studio session, the artist may develop some concepts that you never thought of. Once the artist explains their concept, the producer has to be flexible enough to adjust and quickly reorganize the track to their liking.

Unsigned and aspiring artist can be a great asset for the producer who wants to gain exposure. First of all, the pool of aspiring rappers and singers is so vast that you won't have a problem finding work if you want it. Second, aspiring producers can showcase their production skills to the public through these collaborations. Find the best new artist that fits your style of production and try to make it happen together. It's a win for both parties involved.

One of the funniest types of artists to deal with is the one that just signed a new record deal. Can someone say the word "arrogant?" You would think that all new artists would be receptive to collaborating with aspiring producers. In actuality, some new artists totally reject the idea of collaborating with new beat makers and producers. They believe working with aspiring producers gives the perception of still being an amateur. Working with "well-known" producers appears to be more professional, high budget. New artist don't realize that some "well-known" producers look for opportunities to take full advantage of them. Veteran "well-known" producers know that new artists are inexperienced and very eager to make it big. This enables "well-known" producers to charge higher production fees for meager results.

Partnerships

The music business is a tight-knit society that doesn't easily accept newcomers. Aspiring beat makers and producers will have a difficult time breaking into the business without help. You can have an incredible catalog of music but if you want a career in music production, you have to build it by working with others. Beat makers or producers can create thousands of beats, but they really can't break into the business without developing partnerships. Everyone needs some sort of support during all stages of career building. Developing partnerships with rappers, singers, record label executives, deejays, bloggers and other entertainment businesses will be key to navigating your way through the music business and the overall entertainment industry.

A successful partnership is based on trust, integrity and a mutual agreement on a common goal. Partnerships can be made as a written agreement that explains the obligations or it can be agreed upon orally. When deciding on an arrangement, make sure that all parties share the same common goal.

For example, it's not uncommon for beat makers to partner up with aspiring rappers or singers to break into the industry. As I stated earlier, I started my production career by partnering up with rap artist and childhood friend Cam'Ron. We had the same career aspirations. Through our partnership, we were able to launch successful careers as individuals. We made a decision early on that if we focused on making music together, opportunities would follow.

Another example of great partnership opportunities is with businesses not specifically in the area of music. The music business has expanded into areas that include subscription-based online programming, electronic books, video games, fashion and beverage companies. By music being an essential part of almost every entertainment form, the opportunities for beat makers; producers and songwriters continue to broaden. The days of the traditional "record label" business model being the only resource for beat makers, producers and songwriters is extinct. For example, video game companies such as Activision, actively search for background music for games and advertisements.

Production Psychology

Mastering what I call *production psychology* is a major part of becoming a successful producer. A producer has to be aware of artists' styles and working habits to make good music. Being able to understand the artist and what they are trying to communicate is essential to working productively together. The producer should pay attention to facial expressions, verbal and nonverbal communication like body language. A producer being in tune with an artist can lead to a meaningful and long lasting relationship leading to the creation of great music.

On the flip side, being out of sync with an artist and their needs could lead to a failed project and no future work. It's important to vibe and gel with the artist because a great piece of work with one artist leads to possibilities of creating more work with other artists. Production is a word of mouth business, "Who made that beat?" or "who produced that song?" Those questions lead to more work and bigger paydays.

The way you communicate with the artist will have a direct impact on the final musical product. Which is why you have to speak with finesse, clarity and expertise when consulting with the artist about changes, ideas and possible direction. There is a difference between you saying "that was a terrible take" and "I think you can do a better take." You have to remember that the record is a message to their fans. This piece of work represents them and if they feel like you care and have as much invested as they do, you and your opinions will be respected.

Confidence

Artists will build off of your knowledge and be encouraged to follow your musical direction if you are confident in your musical ability and direction. If you don't believe in what you do, how can any artist take you seriously or depend on you for professional advice? Getting an artist to buy into your musical vision is a major part of being a music producer.

When working with someone that doubles as an artist and producer you have to bring your "A" game. Be willing to stand up for your musical opinions and make sure that they are valid. Not being able to support your opinions may cost you your credibility. You also should be skilled enough to create a balance without coming off as arrogant or self-righteous. As a producer you must realize that a lot of artists are thin skinned. In some cases they aren't used to getting negative feedback. It's not your job to go in reviewing everything about artists you may work with; instead, try to perfect what they do to your beat. Arrogance and know-it-all attitudes can look like "hate," and you and your opinions can be dismissed. Learn how to communicate effectively with artists. You are being hired for your musical expertise, your creative vision and your ability to produce a complete project. Producers have to have a strong personality, a strong musical vision and tough skin. When an artist wants your opinion, you have to be able to give a professional one; and that doesn't always mean agreeing or cosigning the artist.

Speaking up, being strong and knowing your craft will only gain you respect. Telling the artist what they want to hear without giving your professional opinion or supportive facts to back up what you say musically, threatens your professional integrity. There is still a fine line between telling the truth and getting the most you can out of the artist. If you don't develop a relationship with the artist that involves mutual respect, they won't trust your opinions and changes that you suggest. Artist treat new records like their offspring. They love and protect them after they're created (another reason why you need to be in the studio while the music is being developed).

Integrity

An equally important characteristic a producer must have is integrity. If you don't respect what you do it will be hard for others to respect your work. As a producer or beat maker, you have to stand firm when it comes to your musical direction and opinions. If you don't think something is good, then say it. If you think an artist's verse is terrible, lacking in substance or style, it's important that you express your views early. Of course you still have to exercise professional courtesy and be mindful of the artists feelings and sensitivities. But don't let that be a deterrent for delivering the honest truth. When you personally lack integrity, you are also compromising the integrity of your project as well. If you're not honest with an artist, he or she may take control, take the project in the wrong direction and possibly destroy a good concept. Exhibiting confidence in your vision will make you a stronger professional as well as a respected one. Your view and opinions on matters may not be correct 100% of the time but as long as you can support your opinion with evidence and reason, you will gain the respect of the artist you're working with.

Manipulation

Manipulation is a key element to producing good music. Now the word "manipulation" seems negative but it's not. The definition of manipulation is to manage or utilize skillfully. In terms of the beat game, this means getting the artist out of their comfort zone. As a producer, your job is to elevate artists' performances to their highest levels. That includes making all the necessary adjustments to make the project a success. You want to show them a different vision and have them become receptive to your ideals. Sometimes you need to manipulate an artist to get them out of their comfort zone.

Common Ground

Finding a common ground is last but definitely not least. Common ground is the basis of artists and producers relationships. You must find what you and an artist have in common: a common idea or theme that you can build from. Walking into the studio knowledgeable about an artist and their craft will give you the ability to determine several different creative directions.

Your job will be a lot easier if you're working with someone who has a body of work that you appreciate. If that's not the case, try to understand what the artist wants to accomplish. This will give you a better working atmosphere and create a foundation for you to build from. Understanding an artist will allow you to put forward the best product possible. Learning the different players means effective communication. This will allow you to pull from the artist musically. You have to approach each artist differently pulling his or her best talents from them to make good music. Similar to a coach of a basketball team trying to lead the players to a win, a producer's goal is to guide the artists into making a great song. While coaching, you need to be equipped with unique ways to communicate with each individual player to get the best performance. The same rings true in the beat game.

The Grey Area

Building a personal relationship with an artist can provide a huge advantage for an aspiring producer. The greatest advantage is having a direct connection between you and an artist. No A&R representatives, label executives or managers will be in the way to intercept your calls or emails. An artist and producer being able to communicate on a personal level have achieved some of the greatest music ever created. Nowadays, most producers collaborate with artist for free in hopes of landing a placement in the future. Who would turn down access into Lil Wayne's studio? Who would pass on a chance to do several tracks for Lil Wayne? If Lil Wayne is working on an album, one of your tracks could be chosen for the album. Creatively, it's a win-win situation for all parties involved. You go in the studio, create the songs, wait for your check and that's it right? At the end of the day, it's all about the music right? Can it be all so simple? Nope. It's not that easy.

"The Grey Area" is a specific time that usually occurs after all the creative work has been completed between you and an artist. This is the time when everything seems to be at a standstill, and as a producer, you are unaware of what will happen next. The artist and record label are in a great position because they are able to obtain a catalog full of songs, essentially for free. No payments have been made, no final decisions have been rendered and no contracts have been signed leaving the producer is in limbo. Now what if they never use your track? Do you still shop it? What if they don't communicate their intentions for the record but the track was previously on a beat CD and somebody called ready to pay for the track? What do you do then? Sell it for money or hold out for hope? You have to continue to work hard no matter what.

Grinding and Paying Dues

The entertainment industry has a way of making people believe success happens overnight. How many times have you heard a song by a new artist and thought, *where did he or she come from?* We use terms like "overnight success" or "one-hit wonder" to describe artists or producers who we perceive to have experienced success prematurely. The question shouldn't be where did he come from but rather "how did he get there?" Take for instance former New York Knick player Jeremy Lin. People responded as if Lin popped out of nowhere and just started winning games for the Knicks. In all actuality Lin had played his rookie year with the Golden State Warriors before being waived. He played in the D-leagues before being signed as a free agent by the Knicks. Success isn't just receiving a positive result but rather it is the process of receiving positive results through hard work. Success equals hard work combined with luck and personal skill. Hard work is evidenced by dedication, determination, some form of mastery and persistence. When a person reaches some level of success you will be able to follow a trail of hard work, luck and skill in association with that success. You might be asking why I mentioned luck when describing reaching success. Have you ever heard somebody say, "Your timing was just right," "his timing was impeccable," or "you were right 'on time'?" When people speak of timing regarding success or an achievement, they are referring to luck.

If J. Cole wasn't standing outside the building when Jay Z was entering, he could have never handed Jay Z his CD. If you weren't at the grocery store when Dr. Dre was running in real quick you would have never made that initial connection. If you put out music at the wrong time it can be detrimental to record sales but when the timing is right, life is good. Timing is everything! Timing doesn't mean anything if you don't have skill and work ethic. Some things in music may come easy to you but it still takes hard work and dedication to get a complete product that someone else will deem worthy of paying for. If you don't work hard there is very little that luck can do for you. I'm not saying you can't sell a beat that you made in ten minutes. What I am saying is that you most likely won't be making a career out of it.

Hard work is necessary, luck is important and personal skill is essential. "There are two types of people in this world, the ones that watch things happen and the ones that make things happen."[xxxvi] Anyone who has been in the music business knows you have to finance your own career. Your career as a beat maker or producer doesn't start and end with the purchase of your production equipment. You have to invest in this music game. Technology is ever changing and to keep up you must change with it. Hard work, persistence, dedication and constant education are what grinding and paying dues are all about. You earn the right to success and wealth after you exhibit these traits.

Motivation - What's Driving You?

Motivation is the key to life. Motivation means having drive, influence or the desire to do things. It's an emotion that creates a desire within someone to take a course of action whether it's grueling or painstaking. It's the difference between working all night in the studio or going out to a club. Some people are motivated to make music while others will simply dance to it. Some people are motivated to exercise and lose weight while others are stuck in front of the television "snacking." People fail because they don't act. If you become complacent and never push yourself, how can you achieve greatness? Motivation is knowing what you want and then setting goals to attain it. Nobody says that trying to reach your goals won't hurt; just know that it will pay off. Knowing what you want, setting high standards and reaching your goals will undoubtedly be painful but you must be uncomfortable sometimes in your quest for success. People set out to do great things all the time but it's the follow-through and commitment that produces results.

In this industry, motivation is a necessity. You must have the ability to motivate yourself as well as others. Don't get discouraged. Being a producer will have many highs and it will also have lows. You can't let the low times discourage you. You have to believe in yourself and take pride in what you do. Be encouraged about your product and keep your own spirits up. It may sound cliché but you need to be your biggest fan. If you are, you can persuade others and begin to create a team of support for yourself. As a producer you have to motivate people to use your music, you have to keep yourself motivated after your beats don't sell. You must keep yourself motivated when people don't understand your vision. Motivation is a skill and it requires a balance of communication, consistency, determination and structure.

Let's face it, we can all make a New Year's resolution to work out but keeping that goal and losing weight is the bigger challenge. Back in the day, before the Neptune's made it and became household names, they had huge challenges. The Neptunes had great concepts and unique music but new sounds and styles are often times scary for most recording artists. The Neptunes had to get artists motivated to use their tracks. Artists don't like being the first to go out on a limb so some persuading may be necessary. Pharrell pitched his ideas often before having major success with a rapper. They started in the game back in the early 1990s and it wasn't until 1998 with Mase's hit "Looking at Me" and Nore's "Superthug," that they started gaining major success and notoriety. Getting these tracks placed and breaking in their new style wasn't easy in the beginning, but it paid off. I believe that the love for music and the culture kept The Neptunes motivated and determined. If you are developing a brand or a unique style it may not always pay off immediately. The road can be extremely rough at times, but you have to stay encouraged, stay motivated and keep pushing. Remember, a job is something you do for money, but a career is something you do out of love.

Self-Development

One of the reasons I set out to write this book was to provide beat makers and producers with a resource for learning through self-development. Effective players in the beat game take personal responsibility for their own learning and development. They motivate themselves to gain the information needed to develop not only into great music producers, but also a great people. Pro basketball players spend thousands of hours practicing in the gym and studying film to understand the game better. What will you do as a beat maker to further define your skills?

Self-development is a process that happens in three stages. The first stage is the assessment, the second stage is reflection and the third stage is the implementation. It's easy to pick up a book and read it, but will you take the information and apply it to make yourself a better beat maker? It's very important to be honest with yourself while determining your skill level and areas that need improvement.

Assessment

If drum programming is clearly one of your weaknesses, create some sort of drum programming assessment to measure your levels and progress. Challenge yourself to program a drum sequence only using five random sounds. Trust me, you will be impressed with the information you'll discover about your skill level. As you push yourself harder, ask yourself the following questions: *am I making progress? How do I know? Do I need more practice or professional lessons?* You can't look at your progress with "blinders" on. You have to be honest with yourself to move up to the next skill level. Create a developmental plan and take things step by step. Don't expect to go from a five to a ten overnight. I suggest you make a list and knock off task by task. Before you know it, you'll be on a path to more efficient production and closer to being a ten.

Wu-Tang founder and producer RZA used an unorthodox approach to master his equipment of choice: "You can't give me a machine that I don't know how to make a beat with in one night. When I first learned the SP-1200, I just got it with no manual. In one 24-hour period, with no sleep, I figured it out. "Bring the Pain" came off that machine. That's what makes the RZA be the RZA is that I try to master things". [xxxvii]

Reflection

After assessing your skills, it is critical that you reflect on your results. Think about the results and/or data you have collected about your skill level. Are you happy with your level? Are you exactly at the level you thought you would be? What will it take for you to improve in that particular skill? These are some of the questions you should ask yourself during your reflection period. Make sure you document your results, and any other valuable information in a word processing file to monitor your progress.

Implementation

Once you have assessed your skill level and collected a sufficient amount of data, it is now time to act on developing your areas of weakness. One of the first things you can do to improve your skills is simple: Practice! Don't just practice one or two times per week. Make a practice schedule time that forces your productivity. An aspiring pianist needs to practice their instrument to become better. A beat maker needs to do the same. Implementation also involves a beat maker actively acquiring the resources to gain knowledge. Resources include books, publications, tutorials, videos, conferences, seminars and schools.

Formal Education

I can't count how many times people asked for my opinion on what I believe is the "best" music college or university to attend. While some schools may offer a wide variety of music and business courses, the "best" schools are institutions which design a curriculum that prepare students for real careers within the music industry. It won't be sufficient just to enroll in a few music and business courses hoping to receive a well-rounded education in music. The more effective schools will offer courses specific in your areas of interest. My Alma mater, The University Of New Haven offers courses on topics such as music publishing, artist management, record production, copyrights and more.

Attending college or trade school for higher education is essential but it should not be a replacement for your own independent learning. You must take initiative by reading books, doing online research, attending workshops and designating time to work on your craft.

You may experience some discomfort during the three-stage process, which is perfectly understandable. The earlier you begin to evaluate yourself the faster the process will be. If you are honest with yourself while evaluating your progress, your skills will progressively get better. When you get discouraged during the process, remember this quote by Jim Rohm. "Formal education will make you a living. Self-education will make you a fortune." [xxxviii]

Here is a list of a few tips to follow while on the path to self-development:

1. Have a vision and a plan.
2. Read anything you can get your hands on.
3. Learn an instrument.
4. Engage in intellectual activities.
5. Continue (formal) education.

Goal Setting

If you are truly serious about a career in Hip-Hop music production, you need to make everyday a steppingstone towards reaching your goal. The problem is we don't create realistic goals. It's easy to say my goal is to become a "platinum selling music producer" but how do you expect that to happen? When do you expect it happen? Are you putting forth the proper effort to make it happen? If you set a goal for your career and future but aren't motivated to follow the steps in the process, you haven't set an effective goal.

The first thing you need to ask yourself is if your basic goal is realistic. If you want to become a professional NBA player but you haven't developed all the necessary skills in shooting, ball handling, and passing, you can't expect to be among the best basketball players in the world. The same rings true in Hip-Hop production. If your goal is to produce a song for Jay Z, how are you going to realistically make that happen? Is it realistic to think it will happen without a clear plan of how you will make it happen? Jay Z will not be knocking on your bedroom door looking for you. He won't be running up on you at a party. Create a goal that is attainable. A more realistic goal would be: "to initiate contact with the A&R department at Roc Nation within the next 30 days." This would move you towards your ultimate goal.

The second thing you need to ask yourself is how specific is your goal? What exactly do you want to accomplish? You should know in detail what you want to do, when you want to do it and why you want to do it. If your ultimate goal is to produce a track for Jay Z, then you need to find out who is the person who handles music production for Jay Z.

This may become a challenge.

Finally, you should figure out how to measure the progress of this goal over a time period. If you noticed in my Roc Nation example, I added a time frame of 30 days in which the goal needed to be accomplished. Deadlines are really good motivators. Without a deadline, we usually procrastinate until the last minute and produce negative results. If you can measure your progress each week, you'll be able to make the necessary adjustments to achieve your overall goal by the end of the 30 days. In our Roc Nation example, a good addition to the goal would be to add a specific amount of hours you will dedicate towards gaining contact with the A&R department. Remember that achieving your goal might have smaller accomplishments before you reach the final goal. You might reach the A&R and land on another artist's album. That's a goal you didn't count on but an accomplishment just the same.

Finally, after you carefully added all the specifics into your goal, your goal statement should looks something like this:

"My goal is to initiate contact with the A&R Department at Roc Nation by spending at least 7 hours per week researching over the next 30 days."

Fear (The Motivation Killer)

Fear is an emotion that alters the decision making of many of us. Fear can make us lose our motivation. We all have been put in difficult situations where we had to make decisions based on an unknown result. Its easy to make a decision when you believe you know what the end result will be but it becomes more difficult when the result is unknown. The fear of the unknown is scary. I've heard legendary soul singer Sade say that she never collaborated because she always avoided working outside of her safety zone. 99 percent of horror movies are based on the "fear of the unknown." If I asked you to open a mysterious black door, you might be a bit apprehensive about what could be on the other side. That's how some of us feel about success. We're scared of success and what it may bring towards us.

The feeling of success or high achievement is what we all desire but the path in which it takes to reach success is the hardest obstacle for most people to overcome. For example, most producers want to experience having a number one hit song. In the end the opportunity is lost because they spend so much time complaining about the difficulties of making it a reality. Imagine if you spent that time creating opportunities for yourself? If you continue to search for problems, you will eventually find them. Instead, I suggest you stay motivated and work with a purpose. That purpose should be: to build a solid career and working towards professional growth.

Procrastination

You must keep your motivation high to complete tasks promptly. If not you will fall victim to procrastination. Procrastination deters you from reaching success. Everyone suffers from this at some point in his or her life. How many times have you put things off or not done what you set out to do to accomplish your goal? It's easier to make excuses for why things aren't happening for you rather than stepping up and dealing with the work that's ahead of you.

NBA star Allen Iverson became famous for his statement "we are talking about practice" referring to why he did not attend practice. Though I disagree with his disregard for practice, too much practice can sometimes lead to procrastination of getting your work out there. Although practice and skill development are very important in any field, some of us get caught up in being so perfect that we never really move forward. We become slaves to perfection. We spend so much time perfecting our craft that we lose our sense of purpose. If you spend too much time practicing, you will never be able to know how it feels to play in the game. I've heard many great producers (including myself) say how they hate listening to their own songs because they hear things that could be improved. I understand now the importance of letting your greatness shine and displaying your talents.

Instead of beating myself up mentally, I understand that once I reach my point of perfection, all I have to do is let the music go to the world to experience success. Some people don't concentrate on practice they instead focus on going through the motions, which could also hinder them from reaching success. By the motions I mean going through a set of procedures that exemplify the process to success. You know the type: one who spends lots of time in Guitar Center or Sam Ash; a beat maker who has every piece of production equipment known to humankind but hasn't created a beat that anyone enjoys. They're also the beat makers who spend much of their time "building" or "constructing" a studio. So much so that the construction process is more of an ongoing job than making music is. How about the one who copies the process that works for Timbaland, Swizz Beatz or Dr. Dre but has never developed his or her own routine or rituals? Don't get caught up in the dream of making beats to where you never experience the actual reality. Keep your eyes on the prize and focus on the ultimate goal, which is becoming a professional, creating good music and getting paid for it.

Networking

You've heard it before; IT'S ALL ABOUT WHO YOU KNOW! I like to look at it a bit differently. I think it's all about who you don't know. The people that make things happen behind the scenes are the people you need to know. Many of us could recognize celebrities if they were walking down the street but what are the odds of that happening? Depending on where you live, you might not ever see a celebrity in your lifetime. If you are in a major city like New York, Los Angeles or Miami it's very possible but if your plans are to drive around the city like paparazzi, you're in for a long ride. Even if you do get the opportunity to get your music directly into Jay Z's hands, it doesn't necessarily guarantee your "big break" in the industry.

The key is to position yourself to have many opportunities to "break in" instead of waiting for the "big break." "Networking" or "Network" is a term that refers to a social structure made of individuals who are tied to a specific interest. The music industry is a network (although film and fashion industries are applicable to). So, when we talk about breaking into the business, we're really talking about joining the network. This is probably the biggest hurdle or obstacle to overcome. The music industry network is very large and as I mentioned earlier, the people behind the scenes are the ones that will help gain entry into the network. When I say "behind the scenes," I'm referring to anyone within the industry other than the actual artist or celebrity. This includes music executives, publishers, songwriters, assistants, friends and even interns.

Beat makers and producers can benefit tremendously by networking. Networking is one the most valuable uses of your time in terms of the return. If you attend 2 to 3 industry events per week, you can potentially built a good network base, which can lead to future opportunities. Networking at events provides beat makers and producers with the opportunity for face-to-face interaction with like-minded people. If you attend events on a consistent basis, you may create lasting impressions in the minds of the people you meet. People should know your name, recognize your face, and be able to identify your music. The only name you should have to drop is your own.

CEO Syndrome (Business Approach)

The Hip-Hop music industry provides an environment that encourages entrepreneurship. Any individual with a creative mind and strong work ethic can form a business that provides products and/or services. Beat makers or producers can launch a business based on music production services. The feeling of being in control of your own destiny is gratifying if you're willing to put in the work. Beat makers or producers need to be able to wear multiple hats taking on the responsibility of being both beat maker/producer and the C.E.O.

C.E.O. (acronym for "Chief Executive Officer") is the job title of an individual responsible for running and operating a business. The CEO is also responsible for the success or failure of the business. Being the leader of a business is much more than a title. In Hip-Hop music, being a C.E.O. is glorified as a huge status symbol. The perception of being "in charge or "in control" has overtaken much of how some beat makers and producers approach business.

"I'm C.E.O of my company," "I'm the boss," "I'm representing Joe Blow productions" are common phrases thrown around in public. The "I'm the boss" attitude can overshadow the main purpose of the business. Not to mention, if you don't have paid employees being the boss just means you're self-employed with more responsibility.

To become a legitimate C.E.O, one must own or operate a corporation registered within a county of the state they plan to do business in. Setting up your business as a corporation or sole proprietorship is a necessary step for all musicians. I know it sounds cool to call yourself the "CEO" or to feel like you're in the same class as a Sean "Diddy" Combs, Jay-Z or Russell Simmons. Yet, some of us are doing business without owning a corporation. That's like Bill Gates being the head of Microsoft without his business being legally incorporated. That would be unbelievable. Chris Rock once joked and said "Music kind of sucks. Nobody's into being a musician. Everybody's getting their mogul on."[xxxix]

Although I disagree with his view, Rock's point is well taken. Today, beat makers and producers should take business matters into their own hands, but being the C.E.O. is much more than a title. "Artists, lyricists and producers should think of themselves as small labels and publishing companies. Don't rely on someone else to make it happen, you have to be willing to do it for self" says attorney Ian Waldon.[xl]

Finding an even balance between your responsibilities, as a C.E.O. and beat maker and/or producer should be your ultimate goal. After all, these two responsibilities go hand and hand. Successful beat makers and producers create great music and should be effective business people. Don't get consumed by the corporate mentality that may get you away from developing your art.

Paying Your Taxes

After setting up your corporation with your local county clerk's office, your next step should be to register your business with the Internal Revenue Service (I.R.S.). The I.R.S. will always be your silent business partner and as beat maker, you can't ignore paying state and federal taxes on your income. As a United States citizen, we are required by law to do so and being a beat maker is no exception. Even if you're not making a profit, you should get yourself into the habit of keeping financial records and filing tax forms, both as an individual and business owner. Keeping your financial situation organized will most likely prevent any issues in the future. You should definitely consult with a tax professional or accountant to make sure you are handling your finances properly.

As a rule, you should put aside at least 30% of your income in a separate bank account for tax purposes. This money will cover your yearly tax fees when it comes to collection time. It's important that you have discipline and not be tempted to touch this money no matter what. If you were working for any another company, they would automatically take taxes out of each check. Do the same for yourself. If nothing else motivates you, keeping money in your pockets should.

Industry Hygiene

"In business you don't get what you deserve, you get what you negotiate."

Have you ever heard the phrase: "one hand washes the other?" Have you heard someone say, "You scratch my back and I'll scratch yours?" If these anatomy references disgust you, toughen up because these phrases touch on a vital part of how the music production business works. I know you have heard it a million times but I'll say it again: THIS IS A BUSINESS! People couldn't care less how talented you are and they definitely won't do anything without getting something back in return. So, the question is, what would you give up in return for a placement?

Industry Hygiene is a term that I created to describe the act of corruption and bartering that goes on in the music industry. Some of us want to get into this industry to strike it rich but most of us just want to make sure we get paid for the work we do.

The Barter System

While we all expect to get "paid" in dollars or by some other monetary system, there is part of the music economic system that uses bartering as a way of payment. The barter system is the concept of exchanging goods and/or services for other goods and/or services. It's a great way to do business and negotiate agreements without exchanging money. You have to be very careful when using the barter system because what might seem like a simple business transaction could turn into a form of extortion.

If you are a beat maker landing your first major production placement, be prepared to take the ride of your life. Your production work becomes a valuable asset and people will do anything to get a piece of your production credit, copyright or publishing share. I'm not talking about people putting a gun to head (though I've heard about some violent altercations); I'm talking about the threat of you losing out on an opportunity. If I told you I could get you a placement on a 50 Cent record but you would have to give me 50% of your publishing share what would you do? If 50 Cent didn't want to pay you for a track because he was providing you with the opportunity and exposure of being on his album, would you do it?

What about this scenario: Let's say you produced a song for artist A. Artist A decides to get a mega star to feature on the song with him. The mega star doesn't write any lyrics or contribute production. After the song was completed, the mega artist wants part of the publishing share and production credit on the song. Would you agree with that arrangement? Remember, whatever comes out of artist share will come out of your share too. In some cases, you could be asked to give up almost 100% of your contribution in the song. These are real life situations that I've witness or even been in myself.

A few years ago, the former governor of the state of Illinois Rod Blagojevich was removed from his post because of accusations of corruption, conspiracy and taking bribes for Obama's vacant Senate seat. While some of the details are sketchy, we do know that the former governor is guilty of using the barter system to do government business, which is against the law. You can't force an organization to make a financial contribution to your campaign to fund a state run hospital. However, it's not against the law to be pressured or coerced into exchanging a percentage of your publishing for a major production placement. It may not be fair, but it's still a major part of the inner workings of this wonderful music industry.

Have you ever wondered how or why some of these mega stars feature on a new artist record? What about how an A-list producer provides production for your favorite artist? Do you really think Jay Z is going to pay Dr. Dre $250,000 for a track? Do you think Dr. Dre is going to pay Jay Z $250,000 to be on Detox? If you don't know the answer, it's no. If you feature on my song, I'll feature on your song. No harm no foul, the barter and trade system at work.

The most important thing you should get from reading this is the importance of understanding your value. Some people will offer you pennies while others might offer you an opportunity of a lifetime. It's going to be up to you to make the right decision that's best for you and your work. Most of all don't be so naive to think that you will be compensated fairly. In business you don't get what you deserve, you get what you negotiate.

Success

Creativity and success go hand in hand. Success is defined as achieving ones objective and desired outcome. For an aspiring beat maker, success could mean making two beats per day. For a more determined beat maker, success could mean finally getting his or her music into the hands of a major record label A&R rep. The greatest successes in life are created slowly and purposely through the quality of work you do each day. Success should only be determined based on your personal activity and effort. Using your own gauge to measure success is the real key to being successful. If you set and accomplish your personal goals, whether big or small, you are being successful.

Cost of Success

People like to look at successful people and say things like "he forgot where he came from" or "he thinks he's too good for us." Why do you think you hear statements like that all the time? Could it be jealousy or envy? Ask yourself how bad do you really want success? How important is success to you? Now what sacrifices will you make in your quest for success? As you gain success, wealth and wisdom, you will find the need to distance yourself from friends and acquaintances of the past. Yes, they're going to play the "sympathy" card or the "we've been down with you since "day one" cards but changes will have to be made. Successful people don't make it by chance. They have to take appropriate steps to get to the top and sometimes its not so pretty. You have to rid yourself of dead weight. Sometimes old friends bring old habits along for the ride. They aren't up for positive change. You can't fight to become successful and let a friend get you arrested for having a gun in the car or drug possession. Your drug should be success. Get rid of problems don't help create them.

The Art of Negotiation

Good negotiation skills will help you during business transitions and in your everyday life as well. We negotiate with ourselves about basic things. We evaluate products to determine if they are good or not. We make many decisions based on if we believe the outcome will be fair or acceptable based on our own values. When many of us think of negotiation in business, we think we need to be hostile, aggressive or act belligerent to gain a winning edge. The truth is, such attributes do harm during negotiations. The best negotiators focus on making sure that all parties are being treated fairly and both come out winners. When negotiating, you should always have a clear head, listen and think things through.

Most beat makers and producers will be faced with negotiation situations that involve producer fees, publishing shares, royalty percentages, and production credit among other things. The way you approach the situation can certainly determine whether you have a positive outcome. Before you begin a negotiation, think about a starting point. There is need no to focus on areas of a situation that will cause extreme disagreement early on. Focus on the areas that both parties agree on first. For example, if you are negotiating a publishing share, start with a percentage amount that would put each party in somewhat of an advantageous position.

Below are a few techniques that have worked for me while negotiating fees and deals:

1. *Be sure of yourself.* Don't be intimidated by someone's status or ego. You have to enter the room confident and full of authority. If people sense weakness, you may lose your ability to control the conversation and or negotiation. Speak clearly, concisely and don't move too fast. Sometimes when we talk to fast we say something we didn't intend to. You don't want to put all your cards on the table if you don't have to. While negotiating, you want the folks across the table to reveal all of their plans and budgeting details. You have to listen and speak in response to

questions or suggestions. After all, you don't want to talk yourself out of money. Be patient and let things naturally fall into place.

2. ***Be prepared.*** Walk into the room equipped with knowledge. Never go into a situation unprepared. You must know the artist, their music style, their background, the moves they are making and more importantly how they can affect you. If the person is saying they don't have a deal just to get a lower rate, that's not fair to you. If you've done your research you will know their status. They may have signed a deal but decided to keep it quiet for budget purposes. They may also be trying to pay you pennies to save money for the big named producers. If they want your product, they should be willing to pay for it.

3. ***Know your worth.*** Only you know your value. People will always try to get a deal or a discount but do they deserve it? How much do they really want your services, how much do you want to be on their project? Would working on their project benefit you or advance your career? Does their project compromise your integrity or diminish the value of your brand? Are their skills a good match for your production? Do they need you more than you need them? If you decide to work with them keep some type of advantage. Never be afraid to let somebody know that you have options. You don't want to seem obnoxious but if you have multiple people interested in your beats, put potential buyers on notice. They must know that it won't be around forever and if they pass up their chance, it might be gone the next time they reach out to you. If they don't bite, you must not be afraid to walk away. You can't be willing to accept anything that people throw at you because once you do, they'll test you every opportunity that they get. If you accept $500 for a track when you know you shouldn't have accepted less than $1500.00, it will be your royalties next that get devalued. People will try to cheat you out of credits and out of splits, which mean your back end money is compromised. Take a stand up front and you won't regret it later.

4. ***Start high.*** When negotiating, start at the maximum dollar amount that you think is possible. In a case where you're negotiating pay, you have to start high so you can end up where

you really wanted to be. If you are used to getting $2,500.00 a track you might want to start at $7,500.00. Starting at $7,500.00 may get you in a $3-4K range. However, you must be careful not to overdo it. Don't price yourself out of a placement. You don't want to have someone open the door and await your exit from his or her office because of your fee request. You have to feel the situation out, know whom you're dealing with and what their budget is. If they don't have the funds, you can request all you want; but broke is broke.

5. ***Think of alternatives.*** Someone may not be able to meet your financial request but they may be able to provide you with some other alternatives to compensate you for your work. Think of what's on your plate and what you need goal wise. Perhaps you're working with a rapper and he can't pay the full cost for your production work. You want to work with him and he wants to work with you. A solution might be getting him to feature on a record with one of your artists. This may end up being more valuable than you know especially if the artist takes off and becomes a success. You would benefit in two ways, you worked on his project, which gave him positive exposure, and he's now on your artist's project, which would undoubtedly give your artist exposure. Maybe you want to be an artist as well but your writing skills may not be so great. Have the artist you're considering working with to write you a song, a verse or two. Think of alternatives that would benefit you or some interests that you have. Money is the goal because we all have to eat but there are other things that could be potential gold mines you just have to be creative and resourceful.

6. ***Be a salesperson.*** When negotiating, you're working to get the best deal possible for yourself in a business transaction. Negotiation by definition is a mutual discussion and arrangement of the terms of a transaction or agreement. When you are in that room, trying to get your going rate, you have to sell yourself as we previously discussed. You have to toot your own horn and remember whose the customer. They are there for your expertise and professional gift in most cases. You must be able to list your achievements, your current and future projects while clearly stating your vision. As a producer, when making a record you generally have something in mind for that piece of music. You have ideas on what the hook should sound like, if it's an R&B

song or a rap song. Be prepared to articulate your vision, convince the artist that they can carry it out all while promoting yourself and your credentials. Nobody said it was easy but these are some tips that will help you get the dollar amount you're searching for.

7. ***Be flexible.*** Don't walk into a meeting unwilling to negotiate. Consider compromises, bend a little bit to achieve a sale. Don't give away your soul but don't walk away from a good deal because you didn't get one little thing. Find a substitution or a middle point and secure the deal.

8. ***Watch your body language.*** Never let them see you sweat, surprised, flustered or excited. Nervous energy is like telling on one's self. Surprise means you don't deserve it or you're not used to it so the buyer might take the offer back. It translates to; you want this deal so bad you will probably take their lowest offer. Giddy energy and acting like you beat them might make somebody want to rescind the deal. If you're excited about the transaction, maybe you just cheated me. Never make somebody feel like you're the lucky one in the negotiation. The person across the table should always feel like they secured the best deal and they should be walking away on top. If you act like the winner, don't be surprised if they start dodging your calls when it's time to sign a contract.

9. ***Sleep on it.*** Don't rush into any agreement. If you feel pressured, walk away. Many people have lost things that they value because they didn't take the time to think things through. Take your time and don't feel bad about leaving a meeting without having a resolve. The worst thing you could do is to agree with something that hasn't been thoroughly thought through. Be patient, don't force the situation and finally do what's in your best interest.

Game Over?

"The Beat Game" title was derived from my love of basketball and music. Although it is used as a catchy metaphor to market this book, the Hip-Hop music production profession shouldn't be taken lightly. By showing the correlation between the sport of basketball and music production, I hope readers have gained a better understanding of how to be successful. "In music industry, it's similar in that A&Rs, production companies and record companies are always looking for the next new amazing producer talent or trying to figure out how they can work with those superstar A-list producers so that they can work on their recording artists to make hit songs and ultimately sell lots of records" says attorney Matt Middleton.[xli]

What the Future Holds for Hip-Hop Music Production

In the future, I believe producers who aspire to have commercial success will be forced to significantly change to "an artist-first" approach. Major labels will look to sign recording artist who possess the skill as a rapper, singer or musician and as a producer. This is becoming more and more common. "Unfortunately, the bar has been lowered so much in rapping and singing that a producer may have shied away from being an artist before but may feel more inclined to give it a try" says Jerry Barrow. Producer manager Sarah J has a different perspective:

"The urban game is so wide open right now. Artists will use up-and-coming producers for albums these days. The big household producer names are no longer what translates into big sales anymore. It's all about whose bringing a new sound and connecting with the right people who can make things happen." I see fewer opportunities for independent producers to experience commercial success without adapting a more popular format of production. There will be more opportunities for producers to work on projects in independent TV &

film, commercial advertisements, video games, online media, theater and more.

Producers will push the envelope creatively with the use of technology and innovative musical equipment. Journalist Jerry Barrow believes "that a revolution in sample-based production will happen where source material will be altered in more complex ways challenging current copyright law and opening doors to more innovative compositions."[xlii]

In professional sports, most professional athletes desire long-term contract as a form of job security. As an aspiring professional producer, you should desire the same. You need to secure your financial future by generating money from building a catalog and signing your own artist. "There is no long-term contract unless the producer is putting out his own team of artists and he is acting as the General Manager in sports," says Jerry Barrow.[xliii]

No matter what route you take, your success within the music industry will depend on three factors:

1. Creating good music
2. Maintaining your rights
3. Business connections

What the Future Holds for You

Good music will always last the test of time. Keep your focus on being original and resist the temptation of duplicating current musical styles on popular radio. The music that is considered to be classic today embodies the same characteristics; it is innovative, it pushes boundaries of the genre and inspires others. In 1993 on November 9th, two of Hip-Hop's most influential albums were released: "Midnight Marauders" by A Tribe Called Quest and "Enter The Wu-Tang (36 Chambers) by Wu-Tang Clan. In my opinion, these two albums have inspired a plethora of artist and generation of music listeners all around the world.

Your production career will truly depend on whether you

maintain control of your music rights. The entire entertainment industry is built on issuing rights of intellectual properties such as copyrights, trademarks and patents. As a producer, your long-term revenue will be established based solely on the licenses you issue to users. Matt Middleton says:

> Although there are upfront advances for producers as well, as opposed to recording artist, as producers and composers, their main long term revenue streams will stem from music royalties and publishing (i.e. mechanical income, performance income, and generally licensing revenue). As such, the catalogs that they build, the rights that they maintain and the revenue streams that they exploit will dictate whether or not they ultimately achieve real rewards from having successful records on successful projects.[xliv]

Connecting and networking with the right people is a must. Without developing key relationships with the people, you won't get the opportunity to have your music heard. Producer Jake One suggests, "If you make dope beats but don't get the right person on your tracks, you could have a career like a guy who scores a lot of points but doesn't win a thing."[xlv] Networking is also essential because it yields the greatest return in terms of the usage of your time. You can spend a few hours at an industry event and make one connection that may change your professional career. There is nothing better than face-to-face networking because it provides you with the opportunity to leave a lasting impression in the minds of the people you meet. Don't overestimate the value in forming and maintaining a strong contact list. It's imperative and will be your most important asset throughout your career.

Finally, I believe there will be a re-structuring of the traditional music business model, as we know it today. Major record companies will need additional income resources other than selling CDs and digital downloads to maintain profitability. Producers and artists will eliminate the need for record companies by forming their own business partnerships together including members of their Dream Team. There will also be additional members added to the Dream Team. For example, along with your manager, attorney, business manager and close friends, you will now have a publicist, media & technology person too!

Members will handle their responsibilities and as a group and share in all profits.

Conclusion

This concludes the book. I hope you've learned more about Hip-Hop and music production. The cover design of this book was inspired by a basketball coach's clipboard and playbook. You should keep it handy as a reference during your everyday business and production activities. It was also important for me to provide you with the basic framework that can be applied in specific situations. Keep reading this book until the information goes from your short-term memory to your long-term memory. Remember, there are two sides to every story; then there is: The Truth About Hip-Hop Production.

Appendix-**BALL GAME**

My Top Ten Favorite Produced Hip Hop/ R&B Albums:

1) *Off The Wall* - Michael Jackson

2) *The Chronic* - Dr.Dre

3) *Groove Me* - Guy

4) *Doggy Style* - Snoop Doggy Dog

5) *All I Have* - Amerie

6) *Low End Theory* - A Tribe Called Quest

7) *Uptown Saturday Night* -Camp Lo

8) *Enter Da 36th Chamber* - Wu Tang Clan

9) *The Infamous* - Mobb Deep

10) *Reasonable Doubt* - Jay Z

Five Songs That Changed My Life:

1) "Are You That Somebody" - Aliyah

2) "Playing Your Game, Baby" - Barry White

3) "Eric B for President" - Eric B & Rakim

4) "Nobody Beats The Biz" - Biz Markie

5) "Wong" - Al-B and Just Two MC's

My Ten Favorite Producers:

1) Teddy Riley

2) Marley Marl

3) Barry White

4) Curtis Mayfield

5) Dr.Dre

6) Timbaland

7) Burt Bacharach

8) DJ Premier

9) Gamble and Huff

10) Frankie Beverly

Honorable Mentions

J-Dilla, Sean "Puffy" Combs, Larry Smith, Howie-Tee, Pete Rock, Q-Tip, R Kelly and Raphael Saadiq.

Five Pieces of Equipment That Changed My Life

1) Foster 4-Track Cassette Recorder

2) Casio SK-1 Sample Keyboard

3) Mattel Synsonic Drum

4) Akai S900 Sampler

5) Akai-MPC 3000

ABOUT THE AUTHOR

I'm a creative, adaptable and versatile music producer and educator with over 17 years of successful experience in the music industry. During my career as a producer I have worked with major recording artists such as Jay-Z, Beyonce, 50 Cent, Jennifer Lopez, Cam'Ron and Busta Rhymes and have made significant production contributions to recordings that have sold in excess of 30 million. I've developed a music business and technology program that has been used in New York City Public Schools since 2008. I've also founded Producers Skill Inc., and its subsidiaries: Pskill University, MusicBizKids and OnlineBeatTutor.com - all extremely useful tools for aspiring young music producers and executives. My work is dedicated to providing platforms for students to learn and experience different aspects of the music industry whilst developing their musical craft.

Index

Notes

[i] Michael Eric Dyson, *Know What I Mean "Reflections On Hip Hop"*, (New York: Basic Civitas Books, 2007), chap. 7.

[ii] Zock, (One third of Cookin Soul), interview by Darrell Branch, E-mail to author" Cookin Soul," 11 19, 2012.

[iii] Don Cannon, (Producer), interview by Darrell Branch, "Don Cannon Interview," Record, 06 06, 2012.

[iv] Sarah J, (Manager), interview by Darrell Branch, E-mail to author" Sarah J," 05 22, 2012.

[v] Interactive One. "An Exclusive Interview with Love and Hip-Hop's Yandy Smith." WKYS.com. http://kysdc.com/2631602/an-exclusive-interview-with-love-and-hip-hops-yandy-smith/ (accessed April 26, 2012).

[vi] Tony Perez, (Manager), interview by Darrell Branch, E-mail to author "Tony Perez Interview," 12 12, 2012.

[vii] Passman, Donald. *All You Need To Know About The Music Business.* New York: Free Press, 2006.

[viii] Nottz, (Producer), interview by Darrell Branch, E-mail to author 05 20, 2011.

[ix] Matt Middleton, (Attorney at Law), interview by Darrell Branch, E-mail to author "Middleton," 11 28, 2011.

[x] Mr. Devine, (Producer), interview by Darrell Branch, E-mail to author "Mr. Devine," 02 09, 2013

[xi] !llmind, (Producer), interview by Darrell Branch, E-mail to author "!llmind," 04 21, 2012.

[xii] Codrea, David. "MSNBC spreads fear and prejudice over gun owner at

Obama event." Examiner.com. http://www.examiner.com/article/msnbc-spreads-fear-and-prejudice-over-gun-owner-at-obama-event (accessed April 27, 2012).

[xiii] Mr. Devine, (Producer), interview by Darrell Branch, E-mail to author "Mr. Devine," 02 09, 2013

[xiv] Buckwild, (Producer), interview by Darrell Branch, Record, 07 07, 2012.

[xv] Jake One, (Producer), interview by Darrell Branch, E-mail to author "Jake One," 01 11, 2012

[xvii] Middleton, 2012

[xix] Illmind, 2012

[xx] Jake One, 2012

[xxi] "Prince Paul Interview: Paying Dues And Handling Business." Crate Kings Prince Paul Interview Paying Dues And Handling Business Comments. http://www.cratekings.com/prince-paul-interview-paying-dues-and-handling-business/ (accessed April 26, 2014).

[xxii] Broadcast Music, Inc. "BMI, music royalty, music publishing, music licensing...." BMI.com. http://www.bmi.com/.

[xxiii] American Society of Composers, Authors and Publishers. "Welcome to ASCAP. The worldwide leader in performance...." ASCAP.com. http://www.ascap.com/ (accessed April 26, 2014).

[xxiv] SESAC Home." SESAC.com. http://www.sesac.com/.

[xxv] Boonie Mayfield (Producer), interview by Darrell Branch, E-mail to author "Boonie Mayfield," 04 13, 2012.

[xxvi] Zock, (One third of Cookin Soul), interview by Darrell Branch, E-mail to author" Cookin Soul," 11 19, 2012.

[xxvii] Jason, . rapbasement.com, "Game Respects RZA Despite Beef." Last modified 03 02, 2011. http://www.rapbasement.com/the-game/020311the-game-says-he-respects-raekwon-dispute-their-recent-feud-over-his-mix-tape-details-here.html.

[xxviii] Langhorne, . "Lil Wayne Finally Works Out A Sweet Deal, Settles $20 Mil "Lollipop" Lawsuit." *sohh.com*, 04 30, 2012. http://www.sohh.com/2012/04/lil_wayne_finally_works_out_a_sweet_de al.html (accessed April 5, 2014).

[xxix] Horowitz, Steven. "50 Cent Sued Over Mixtape Sample." *HipHopDX.com* (blog), April 23, 2012. http://www.hiphopdx.com/index/news/id.19486/title.50-cent-sued-over-mixtape-sample (accessed).

[xxx] Kuperstein, Slava. "Lord Finesse Sues Mac Miller For $10 Million Over "Hip 2 Da Game" Instrumental." *HipHopDX.com* (blog), July 11, 2012. http://www.hiphopdx.com/index/news/id.20375/title.lord-finesse-sues-mac-miller-for-10-million-over-hip-2-da-game-instrumental (accessed).

[xxxi] 730, . HipHopGame.com, "Hi-Tek Interview." Last modified 2008

[xxxii] Lynn Hopson, (Publicist, Hobbiecom.com), interview by Darrell Branch, E-mail to author06 12, 2012.

[xxxiii] Branch, Araabmuzik. Interview by author. Phone interview.

[xxxiv] Sarah J, (Manager), interview by Darrell Branch, E-mail to author" Sarah J," 05 22, 2012.

[xxxv] Boonie Mayfield, 2012

[xxxvi] "Quotes Daddy." QuotesDaddy.com. http://www.quotesdaddy.com/ (accessed April 27, 2012).

[xxxvii] Golianopoulos, Thomas. "Wu Warrior RZA." *Scratch Magazine*, January 1, 2006.

^{xxxviii} Kimbro, Dennis, and Napoleon Hill. *Think And Grow Rich*. New York: Fawcett, 1992.

^{xxxix} Plenty of rappers say, "I'm not a rapper, I'm a businessman."." *Rolling Stone*, November 15, 2007, 157."

^{xl} Ian Waldon, (The Waldon Law Group), interview by Darrell Branch, E-mail to author7 7, 2012.

^{xlii} Barrow Jerry, (Senior Editor of UrbanDaily.com), interview by Darrell Branch, E-mail to author "Jerry Barrow," *Former Editor-in-Chief of Scratch Magazine*, 10 28, 2012.

Bibliography

Baskerville, David. *Music Business Handbook & Career Guide.* 5th ed. Thousand Oaks, Calif.: Sage Publications, 1995.

Lustberg, Arch. *How To Sell Yourself.* New Jersey: Career Press, 2002

Passman, Donald. *All You Need To Know About The Music Business.* New York: Free Press, (2006): 197-299.

THE
BEAT GAME
"The Truth About Hip-Hop Production"

DARRELL "DIGGA" BRANCH

BRANCH FAMILY
PUBLISHING

51108011R00139

Made in the USA
San Bernardino, CA
13 July 2017